Another Year of Good Teammate Musings

LANCE LOYA

ISBN-13: 978-1-7370889-0-5

www.coachloya.com

Design and publishing by Cager Haus.
Cover image by Kutsal Lenger, Dreamstime.com.

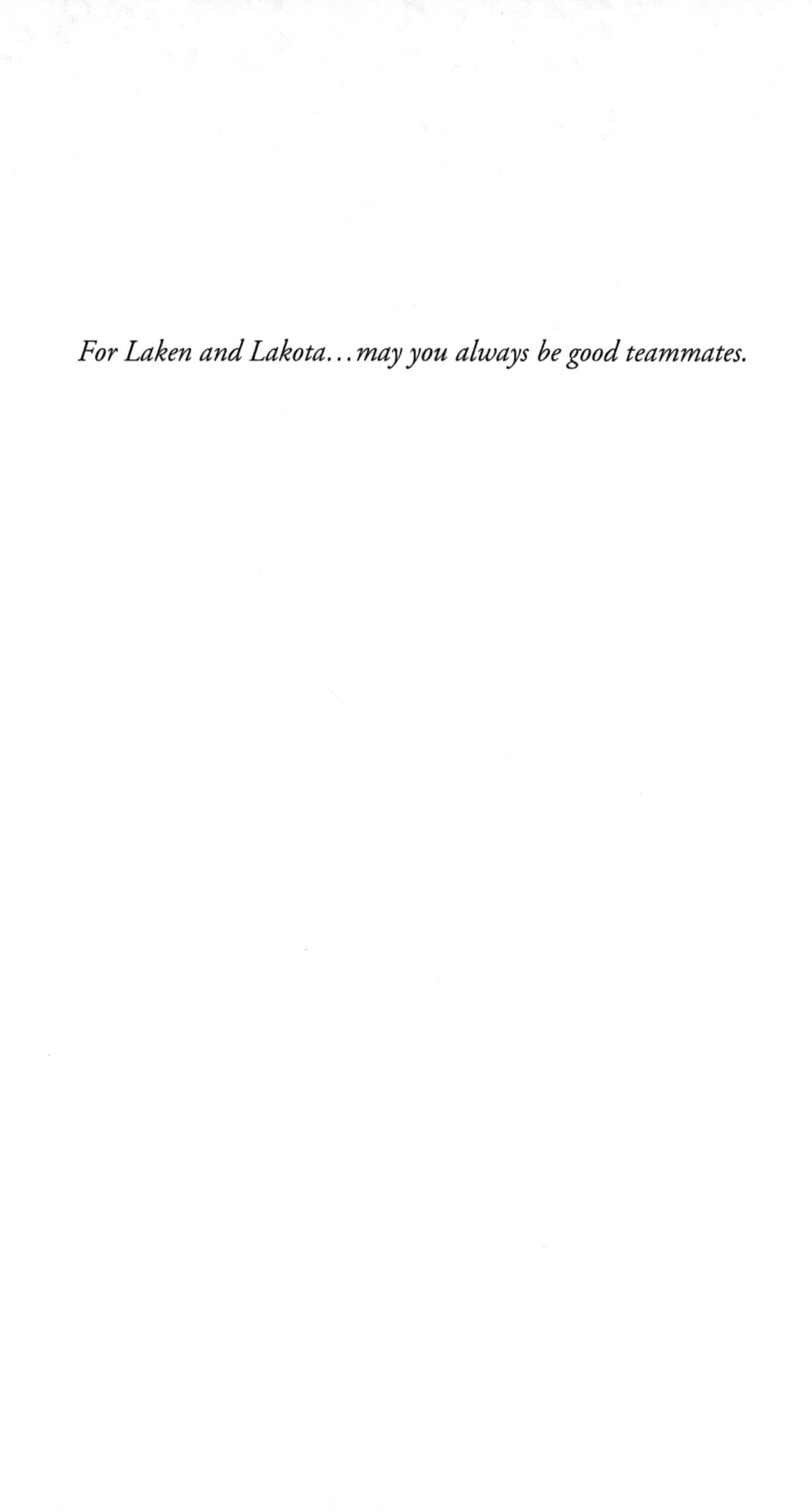

For Laken and Lakota…may you always be good teammates.

Contents

Acknowledgements

A special thank you to Wendy Clouner for suggesting that I start a blog. Although I wasn't initially receptive to your suggestion, I am glad I eventually acquiesced. I also want to express my gratitude to Rachel Loya, Cindy Davis, Jerry Pirrung, and Craig Sikurinec for your continued support and recommendations.

I would also like the thank my Good Teammate Factory clients and the online community members who read blogs, listen to podcasts, like and share posts, and offer invaluable feedback and encouragement. They are the fuel that powers the *Be a Good Teammate* movement.

Introduction

Welcome to *Teammate Tuesdays Volume IV!* Assembling another book of this nature is still surreal to me, as is how this book series came to be.

Once upon a time, I set out on a journey to discover an answer to the question: What does it *really* mean to be a good teammate? Everybody belongs to some type of team. Maybe it's an actual sports team, or maybe it's the place where you work, the community you live in, the church you attend, or simply your family. Ultimately, the success of any team depends on its members' capacity to be good teammates. But what specifically does being a "good teammate" mean?

My journey began with the publication of a children's book called *Be a Good Teammate*. The book revolved around the idea that good teammates do three things: care, share, and listen. I wrote that book with the sole intention of conveying some fatherly advice to my daughters, who, at the time, were learning to read.

The publication of *Be a Good Teammate* unexpectedly set into motion a sequence of events that changed the trajectory of my life and led me to the realization that the world needs more good teammates—kind, mindful, unselfish individuals who put the needs of their teams ahead of their own agendas. This belief transcends sports and applies to all varieties of teams.

The journey eventually brought me to a point where exploring the art of being a good teammate became my life's work. Somewhere along the way, I decided to heed the advice of a trusted friend and share my discoveries—my *musings*—in a weekly blog. I called the blog "Teammate Tuesdays" and posted a new entry every Tuesday morning.

As the blog's following grew, subscribers began reaching out to me about the possibility of making the content available in print form. They wanted to give the blog as a gift to their friends, families, and teams. To accommodate the recurring requests, I turned the entire first year of my blog into a book titled *Teammate Tuesdays: A Year of Good Teammate Musings.*

The book you're presently reading is a compilation of the entire fourth year of my blog. Like the previous volumes, this book will provide you with an abundance of "good teammate" stories, observations, and insights—each intended to make you think about what kind of teammate you are.

The height of the COVID-19 pandemic serves as a backdrop to the year covered in this volume. The virus caused peoples' lives to be changed in ways they could have never imagined. New norms were introduced, forcing many to alter their prior methods of operations. *Adaptability* became an underlying theme to life, as did *prioritization.* As you will soon learn, both of those themes are relevant to the art of being a good teammate.

It should be noted that this book is written in a more informal, conversational tone—the way blogs typically are. Each post (chapter) was written as an independent entity. With a few exceptions, like the removal of embedded hyperlinks and the addition of appropriate citations, the content has not been altered from how it originally appeared online. Sometimes this translates into me repeating a particular word or phrase in consecutive chapters. An editor wouldn't allow this to happen in a traditional book. But I suspect it won't take much effort on your part to see past this type of minor faux pas and still appreciate the lessons.

I like the idea of assembling an entire year's worth of posts in a book format. The content is worth sharing in an alternative medium. Not everyone who can benefit from the message reads blogs. Some people still prefer to hold a physical book in their hands. Putting the blog in book form makes it possible to share the message with a broader audience.

A book is also a convenient way to bring up to speed those who may be joining the Good Teammate movement *already in progress.* The format allows you to experience your own journey of discovery, at your own pace. You don't have to wait until next week to find out what topic I am going to cover in my blog. You can read the chapters as fast or slow as you desire. It's like binge reading a blog.

I am often asked two questions: *Why Tuesdays?* and *Why doesn't the first chapter start on January 1?*

We all have seasons to our lives. For some, it's spring, summer, fall, and winter. For those involved in sports, it's preseason, regular season, postseason, and offseason. I wrote my initial blog post at the end of April, coinciding with what was at that time considered to be the start of my offseason—the ideal time to start new endeavors. I have consistently added a new post every week since then, which is why the first chapter doesn't start on January 1.

Why Tuesdays? I am a fan of Mitch Albom's memoir *Tuesday's with Morrie*. In the book, he chronicles the wisdom acquired from his weekly visits with his former sociology professor Morrie Swartz, who is dying from ALS. The name *Teammate Tuesdays* was a tip of the hat of sorts to Albom's book and its touching premise. But that's not the only reason. I also believe that Tuesdays are generally the best days for personal and professional development.

Wednesdays mark the middle of the week. It's *hump day.* You've come to the realization that you better put your nose to the grindstone and get busy or you're going to run out of time.

Thursdays still have some of the same urgency to get your work done as Wednesdays. But by Thursday afternoon, you are starting to set your sights on the weekend.

Fridays are the day to wrap up loose ends and then coast through the rest of the day. It's the end of the traditional work week, so you're reluctant to start any new projects. You may also feel burned out by Friday and not necessarily motivated to engage in anything mentally taxing.

Saturdays are spent catching up on chores, like cutting grass and doing laundry. Saturdays are additionally a day for recreation and seeking fun.

Sundays are family time. You're ready to relax and spend quality time with your family. If you're struggling with your job, you'll probably spend Sunday evening stressing about having to go back to work the next day. Professional development isn't a high priority on Sundays.

Mondays are consumed with playing catch up. You're trying to finish all the work you didn't complete—but should have—last week. You are probably also being bombarded with everything that was delivered over the weekend. You have an endless amount of pressing emails and phone calls to return. By the time Mondays are over, you are exhausted.

Which brings us to Tuesdays. You are tired from playing catch up on Monday and not anxious to put in another intense day of work. You convince yourself that you still have the rest of the week to get your work done. Why start today? Tuesdays are the perfect day to invest in self-improvement.

Sound familiar? If so, then you've come to the right place. Every day is *Tuesday* in this book.

I hope you enjoy my collection of good teammate musings. My wish is for them to inspire you to become a better version of yourself and to equip you with the tools to help others do the same.

Ten Ways to Stay Connected to Your Teammates

APRIL 28

When you enjoy your teammates' company, being away from them can be hard to handle. If not effectively managed, an extended hiatus will weaken the connection between teammates and hinder the team's chances for future success. The longer the hiatus, the higher the probability of this happening.

Time and distance strain relationships. Sports teams experience this strain during the offseason, as do military marriages and quarantined work colleagues. Relationships that remain strong through periods of separation are the products of intentional actions to counter the interruption.

Good teammates make a deliberate effort to stay connected to the rest of their team during periods of separation. They are proactive in preventing time and distance from diminishing their teams' connectedness. Good teammates understand that connected teams become successful teams.

Here are ten ways to stay connected to your teammates during a prolonged hiatus:

1. Like, love, and share their social media posts. Be it Facebook, Twitter, Instagram, Snapchat, TikTok, or any of the other forums, social media has become an outlet for self-expression. Liking someone's post is the modern-day equivalent of extending a compliment. The appearance of a thumbs up or heart icon validates their presence in your life and lets them know you are paying attention.

2. Text/email them. You don't have to send anything in depth. A simple message letting them know you were thinking about them will suffice. Receiving a "TAU" (Thinking About U) message can be surprisingly ingratiating.

3. Send handwritten notes. This idea may be old-fashioned and a little unusual, but that's precisely why it works. People don't get messages via snail mail the way they once did which makes getting a card unique. Who doesn't enjoy being made to feel *unique*? Not sure what to include in your card? Send a TAU message or draw a doodle inside the card. What you send isn't as important as the novelty of you sending it.

4. Call/Facetime/Skype/Zoom. Written messages are good, but they are void of tone, inflections, and body language. Making the extra effort to sometimes communicate though audio or video allows you to more accurately convey your emotions and reminds the recipient of what a conversation with you is like.

5. Share a photo of a good memory. Communication does not have to be limited to conversations and written messages. Sharing a photo of a good memory can also be an effective way to maintain a connection with your teammates. Photos of good memories elicit emotional responses. Shared emotional responses bond individuals.

6. Share a meme from a movie/TV show you both like. Memes or short clips from movies or television programs you watched with your teammates evoke emotional responses, too—especially if they cause people to "LOL." Funny memes bring back good memories and take advantage of the bonding power of laughter.

7. Share a meal photo. Seeing photos of what others are eating for lunch can grow tiresome. But when you formerly ate lunch every day with that person, it's nice to feel like you're *being kept in the loop*. And for similar reasons as the previous two entries, seeing an occasional meal photo may conjure mutual feelings of nostalgia.

8. Describe a dream or goal you have. Anything that conveys what you envision the future will be like after you are reunited is beneficial. Describing a dream or a goal in detail compels others to think about the future and fosters hope. You inspire your teammates when you discuss your excitement for the future.

9. Reveal a mistake you recently made. Portraying a prosperous online image isn't incredibly difficult to do. But what about what's happening outside of the camera frame? Ironically, masking your flaws can discourage your teammates. If they are experiencing challenges, the prosperous image you're projecting may deter them from sharing their experiences. Revealing a recent mistake shows you're human. Exposing your vulnerability can endear you to your teammates.

10. Acknowledge their milestones. This suggestion may be listed last but make it an absolute priority. Failing to recognize a teammate's birthday, anniversary, or other special occasion will be perceived as more than a slight. If a milestone is important to your teammate, it should be important to you. People remember who congratulated them on their achievements, who wished them happy birthday, and who offered condolences on their loved one's passing. But they also remember who did not—and they aren't nearly as connected to those who did not.

As always…Good teammates care. Good teammates share. Good teammates listen. Go be a good teammate.

The Greatest Teacher, Failure Is

MAY 5

Yesterday was "Star Wars Day." The fan-revered hashtag *#MayTheFourthBeWithYou* trended on social media with the speed of the Millennium Falcon zooming through hyperspace.

I posted a photo on my social media pages of my daughters and I wishing everyone a happy Star Wars Day. In the photo, we all sported our yellow "Be a Good Teammate" t-shirts. My youngest daughter wore a Princess Leia double-buns wig, while her older sister donned a Darth Vader mask.

The photo was cute and appeared to capture a fun family moment. Outside of the camera lens, however, the experience was rather unpleasant.

My daughters were being difficult. They argued over who got to wear the Princes Leia wig and who got to wear the Darth Vader mask. They argued over who got to hold the blue lightsaber and who got to hold the red lightsaber. They didn't like where they were positioned, and they didn't like the way the sun shined in their eyes.

Their behavior reinforced the iconic wisdom of W.C. Fields: *Never work with animals or children.*

The photographer (my wife) was also struggling. She couldn't seem to get the right angle or take the photo without someone's eyes being closed. As if all of that weren't enough, we inadvertently stood on an anthill and were attacked by fire ants.

But the biggest problem with the photoshoot wasn't my daughters. It wasn't my wife. It wasn't the fire ants nor the bright sun. It was me. My lack of patience exacerbated everyone else's problems.

I frequently write about the need for good teammates to confront toxicity on their teams. But occasionally, the need to exercise temperance trumps the need to confront.

Good teammates practice understanding. They appreciate the difference between frustrations caused by ill-intent versus those caused by ignorance or inability. Having high standards and being demanding of our teammates can be counterproductive without practicing understanding.

My daughters weren't trying to be difficult. They lacked the ability to behave more maturely. My wife wasn't trying to take bad pictures. She was working with uncooperative subjects and lacked the experience of a professional photographer.

I needed to be more patient and understanding. My short-tempered reactions had turned me into a bad teammate. I was the greatest source of our team's toxicity. Fortunately, my wife and daughters were better teammates to me than I was to them. They were able to forgive and see beyond my failures.

When I returned to our house to download the photos and treat my ant bites, I started to think about the reason behind our photoshoot—Star Wars.

The Star Wars franchise is loaded with examples of good teammates whose attributes overshadow their shortcomings. Han Solo's courage overshadows his recklessness. R2-D2's bravery overshadows his stubbornness. Rey's compassion overshadows her impulsiveness. Chewbacca's loyalty overshadows his slowness. C-3PO's honesty overshadows his fastidiousness.

My failure in our *#MayTheFourthBeWithYou* experience taught me a valuable lesson: Sometimes being a good teammate means having the patience to see beyond our teammates' shortcomings and value their more prominent attributes. Genuine truth lies in the words of Jedi Master Yoda, "The greatest teacher, failure is."

As always...Good teammates care. Good teammates share. Good teammates listen. Go be a good teammate.

Silhouette Teammates

MAY 12

With the growing number of team meetings conducted through video conferences, a new brand of undesired teammates has emerged—*silhouette teammates.*

Silhouette teammates are individuals who have sunlit windows or other sources of bright light behind them that cause their on-screen image to appear darkened and distorted. As the name suggests, only their shadowy silhouette is visible to the other conference participants.

Speaking from this position is inconsiderate and evidence of a lack of empathy—even when it's done unintentionally. Silhouette teammates aren't considering what it's like to be on the other side of their communications. They're often unaware of how distracting they are and how much more challenging it is to converse with them.

Most experts assert that seventy percent of communication is nonverbal. By positioning themselves in front of light sources and allowing their images to be distorted, silhouette teammates deprive viewers of the opportunity to see their facial expressions and read their body language. Their awkward position diminishes their ability to effectively communicate.

While the label "silhouette teammates" is new, the problem of unempathetic teammates failing to consider how their actions—or inactions—impact the other members of their team is not. Insufficient empathy plagued teams long before the advent of video conferencing.

Good teammates practice self-awareness. They have empathy and are cognizant of how their choices affect the other members of their team. Good teammates factor this valuable information into their decisions before they proceed.

A definitive correlation exists between the depth of a team's empathy and the amount of drama it encounters. Empathetic teams have less drama and are more connected.

I enjoy watching Westerns. A favorite of mine is Clint Eastwood's classic *The Outlaw Josey Wales*. The film is about an aggrieved Confederate soldier who refuses to surrender.

In one of the film's pivotal scenes, Eastwood's character approaches a group of Comancheros who kidnapped his sidekick, an affable old Cherokee named Lone Watie. With the sun rising behind him, Eastwood rides his horse toward the kidnappers. Watie remarks that forcing the Comancheros to face the sun gives Eastwood "an edge."

Having the sun at their back may give gunslingers an edge, but it won't work that way for participants on a team video conference. Being a better teammate will give your team an edge. And being considerate of others and practicing empathy will make you a better teammate.

As always…Good teammates care. Good teammates share. Good teammates listen. Go be a good teammate.

**Want to improve the quality of your team video meetings? Check out this short video we released about the Three P's (Position, Placement, and Presentation) of Video Meetings: https://www.coachloya.com/silhouette-teammates/*

Canned Laughter

MAY 19

If you are anything like me, you've found yourself laughing less than usual at the jokes on late-night talk shows. Yes, the quarantine is forcing the shows to be filmed from the confines of the hosts' homes. And yes, the altered format can be a little unsettling. But the jokes are still good.

The jokes are funny, well-written, and delivered with the same impeccable timing. They're just not eliciting the same laugh out loud outbursts that they previously did.

At first, I couldn't quite put my finger on the reason. But then I happened to catch a replay of an episode of *Curb Your Enthusiasm* where Larry David encounters a "professional crier"—someone theatres hire to sit in the audience and cry out loud during dramatic scenes, thus prompting other audience members to cry.

Even though crying was the opposite emotion, it occurred to me that I wasn't laughing at the late-night talk show jokes because the quarantine shows were missing their professional laughers—laugh tracks. The shows were void of the accompanying canned laughter that I'd grown accustomed to hearing.

Entertainers have long been aware of the influence the sound of laughter can have on an audience. The phenomenon is known as emotional contagion and happens whenever our emotions trigger similar emotions or behaviors in others. We feel compelled to laugh whenever we hear others laugh.

Emotional contagion is why we start to chuckle before we ask someone who's already laughing: "What's so funny?"

A sound engineer named Charley Douglas invented laugh tracks in the 1950s. As the entertainment industry transitioned to television, the need to utilize the emotional contagion brought on by a live audience remained evident.

But live audiences were unpredictable and problematic for television. Sometimes they didn't laugh on cue. Sometimes they laughed too loud. And sometimes they laughed too long, which caused programs to exceed their time allotment. So Douglas began adding a soundtrack of pre-recorded laughter and applause to the television shows he produced.

As he predicted, his shows drew more laughs and had higher ratings. Inserting laugh tracks soon became the industry standard.

Good teammates are like laugh tracks in that we don't realize how influential they are until they are gone. Good teammates are also like laugh tracks in that they compel an emotional response from us. When a good teammate demonstrates enthusiasm, we feel and act enthusiastic. When a good teammate demonstrates optimism, we feel and act hopeful.

The influence they have over our emotions and our actions shouldn't be underestimated. Good teammates are as infectious as any virus. Only their infectiousness won't lead to your demise; it will lead to your triumph.

As always...Good teammates care. Good teammates share. Good teammates listen. Go be a good teammate.

Relentless

MAY 26

During the Q&A portion of a recent webinar I conducted, a participant asked me what one word I felt best describes good teammates. The question proved surprisingly difficult for me to answer.

Good teammates possess so many positive attributes that it's hard to describe them with a single word. Good teammates are enthusiastic, committed, loyal, faithful, etc. How could I pick just one without discounting the significance of all the others? I felt obligated to provide an answer though, so I said *love.*

I briefly explained that good teammates' actions are often motivated by love—love for their team, love for their teammates, and love for the process. Good teammates have love in their hearts. Love seemed like an acceptable response, or at least it did at the time.

After the webinar ended, I started to reflect on my response. Something about it didn't sit well with me. Love is one of those rare words in the English language that can be both a noun and a verb.

Good teammates do have love in their hearts and love is often the motivation behind their actions. But good teammates don't love every aspect of being a good teammate. They don't love having to sacrifice. They don't love having to hold others accountable. They don't love having to confront toxicity. They don't love having to temper their words.

They do those things out of love, but they don't necessarily love doing them. Was love the best choice for my "one word" to describe good teammates?

I obsessed over that question all weekend. Sunday morning, I went for a walk along the beach. I like to walk on the beach. I like the feel of the sand on my feet, the smell of the salty air, and the sounds of the seagulls. My favorite part, however, is the waves. I like to watch the waves when I walk on the beach.

The waves never stop. They just keep coming. Sure, their height and intensity vary with the tides, but the waves never stop. They don't take any breaks. They keep coming, one right after the other, twenty-four hours a day, three hundred and sixty-five days a year. The waves are relentless.

As I watched the waves this weekend, I realized that there is a better word than love to describe good teammates—*relentless.*

Good teammates are relentless. Their enthusiasm is relentless. Their commitment is relentless. Their loyalty is relentless. Even their effort is relentless. They never stop trying to be good teammates.

The positive attributes of good teammates don't take any breaks. Good teammates are always kind, faithful, hardworking, and so on. Their positive attributes and their actions are constant.

Bad teammates rarely exhibit this level of relentlessness. Their actions tend to fluctuate with their team's success. When their team is doing well, they're committed. They treat others kindly and project confidence.

But when their team struggles, their faith wanes. They mistreat others and project apathy. This is never the case with good teammates. Good teammates are defined by their relentlessness. Like the ocean's waves, they just keep coming.

As always…Good teammates care. Good teammates share. Good teammates listen. Go be a good teammate.

Five Ways to Crack the Stranger Barrier

JUNE 2

Good teammates share, and I feel compelled to share a book recommendation this week: *Talking to Strangers* by Malcolm Gladwell. I read this book several months ago, but recent world events have reminded me of its significance and that's why I'm recommending it today.

The book is about the conflicts we invite into our lives because we're unable to make sense of people we don't know. We frequently misinterpret the actions, words, and intentions of strangers in a way we never would of people we know.

Gladwell's book made me think about how this topic applies to the art of being a good teammate. When dealing with a team that is diverse and deficient in familiarity, cracking what I call the *stranger barrier* can be challenging. How can you quickly convey to others that you are a good teammate and that they can be a good teammate to you when you are essentially a stranger to them?

Here are five ways to initiate the process of cracking the stranger barrier:

1. **Smile.** Smiles transcend age, gender, ethnicity, and language. As writer William Arthur Ward said, "A warm smile is the universal language of kindness." Smiles convey kindness and kindness facilitates trust. We don't think of people we trust as being strangers.

But be careful…smiles are subject to additional cultural interpretations. What is viewed as friendliness to some may be taken as nervousness or smugness to others. While a smile is a good start, it requires the support of the rest of this list to be rendered effective.

2. **Use Welcoming Body Language.** Posture, facial contortion, and hand gestures trigger important nonverbal cues. A closed posture (hunching forward with crossed arms and/or legs) suggests defensiveness, unfriendliness, and hostility. Whereas an open posture (body trunk squared with hands relaxed and exposed) suggests friendliness, receptiveness, and sincerity.

But be careful…even with an open posture and welcoming facial expressions, the size and velocity of your gestures can skew the message. Large, fast gestures imply aggression. Small, slow gestures imply tranquility.

3. **Reveal Trivial Details About Yourself.** Humans have an innate desire to categorize. The unknown is

unsettling, so we try to interpret the unknown by categorizing strangers based on their similarity to those with whom we've previously interacted. The flawed process starts by analyzing what we see. Providing information that can't be derived from what is seen broadens the categorization process. For instance, if you tell a someone that you love McDonald's French fries, you trigger a new association. The other person might think, "My Aunt Helen loves McDonald's French fries, too. My Aunt Helen is kind and sweet." Suddenly, you're now placed in the same category as Aunt Helen, and you're less of a stranger than you were before you spoke.

But be careful...revealing information that is too personal or polarizing could lead you to be miscategorized and draw undesired suspicion. Your attempt to broaden the categorization process will backfire. The key is to share trivial details.

4. **Pay a Compliment.** Few things build rapport quicker than receiving positive feedback. We're inevitably endeared to persons who pay us compliments because they make us feel good about ourselves.

But be careful...compliments must be sincere. Offering phony compliments will be counterproductive and cause your intentions to be questioned. You can often deliver sincerity by explaining the source of your compliment. "I love your boots. They remind me of my Uncle Jim. He was the kindest person I ever met, and he used to wear boots like that."

5. **Offer Assistance.** We tend to trust those who demonstrate humility through their willingness to serve. Is there something the other person needs help with? Can you hold the door for the person whose hands are full? Can you offer a tissue to the person who sneezed? Small gestures of kindness signal empathy.

But be careful... For the same reasons as above, a lack of sincerity can bring your intentions into question. Offering too much help too early will make the other person wonder about your motives. Sometimes it's best to remove doubt and state your empathy before offering to help. "You look like you're struggling with that. How can I help?"

The solution to many of our teams' problems—and many of the world's problems too—lies in breaking down the stranger barrier and turning strangers into teammates. When strangers become teammates, we start fighting for each other instead of against each other.

As always...Good teammates care. Good teammates share. Good teammates listen. Go be a good teammate.

Rocketman Regret

JUNE 9

Twenty years ago, I had tickets to see Elton John in concert, but I never made it to the show. I got caught up with work and gave my tickets away—a decision I have long regretted.

I always told myself I would catch him *the next time*. However, *the next time* came and went, and so did the one after that, as did the one after that. Numerous *next times* passed without me attending an Elton John concert.

When it was announced last fall that he would be doing his "final" farewell tour, I decided I needed to right the wrong and put an end to my regret. I bought tickets to a show that was supposed to take place last week. Much to my disappointment, that Elton John show—like many other large gatherings—was postponed. (Curse you, COVID-19!)

Elton John turned 73 in March. The reality is that I may be running out of *next times*. I am hoping a make-up date happens and I finally get to see him perform live. Perhaps as a way of subconsciously coping with my disappointment, I've been incessantly listening to Elton John songs ever since the postponement was announced.

My favorite Elton John song is "Your Song." I'm particularly fond of a line in its refrain: *How wonderful life is when you're in the world.* To me, that line illustrates precisely what it feels like to have a good teammate.

The presence of good teammates creates psychological safety, which allows us to express our thoughts, be creative, and show vulnerability without the fear of ridicule or retribution. Good teammates free us of stressful confines and facilitate happiness. Having them on our team genuinely makes for a *wonderful life*.

Of course, true fans know that Elton John didn't write that line. It was written by Bernie Taupin, his longtime lyricist partner. Having collaborated on over 30 albums, they are by far the most successful songwriting duo in the history of pop music.

Bernie Taupin and Elton John epitomize the word teammates. Their success is propelled by a potpourri of mutual respect, admiration, and unwavering commitment. Their talents are complimentary, making them a perfect example of synergy.

"Your Song" was Elton John's first big hit. His top grossing hit is "Candle in the Wind." Ironically, those two songs address the most compelling aspects of being part of a team. "Your Song" details the joy of being around good teammates. "Candle in the Wind" details the horror of being surrounded by bad teammates.

Letting your guard down is impossible around bad teammates. Psychological safety is nonexistent. Bad teammates leave you feeling isolated, *never knowing who to cling to when the rain sets in.*

Elton's John biopic, *Rocketman*, ends with Taron Egerton, who portrays Elton John, singing "I'm Still Standing." Maybe that's an appropriate way to end this blog, as it is often the marching anthem/mantra of a good teammate. When adversity strikes, good teammates are the ones still standing. They aren't deterred by setbacks and they never abandon their team.

As always...Good teammates care. Good teammates share. Good teammates listen. Go be a good teammate.

Smiling Eyes

JUNE 16

Good teammates listen with their ears and their eyes—meaning they maintain direct eye contact with the speaker while providing emotional feedback through facial contortions in the area around their eyes. I had an experience with a grocery store employee named Chris that reminded me of the significant role our eyes play in effective communication.

I was at the store on a busy Saturday morning. The checkout lines were longer than normal, so I had an opportunity to observe Chris bag the groceries of several customers in front me. I was impressed with her exceptional courtesy. Chris's store is known for offering superior customer service, but her welcoming demeanor was extraordinary by even their standards.

When it came my turn to check out, Chris greeted me with the same warm sincerity. Although she was wearing a face mask, I could tell Chris was smiling. I could see it in her eyes. For those working in service industries, masks can be inhibitors to quality interactions with customers. But Chris proved that does not have to be the case.

Chris's courtesy extended beyond the store's customers. A teenager working the cash register was obviously new to his job. He wasn't sure how to enter one of my items and asked Chris for help. She politely, and patiently, provided him with the necessary instructions. Her eyes smiled the entire time. Chris's attitude was contagious.

I pushed my cart towards the parking lot and left the store in a good mood. Chris was a big reason for my happiness. As I unloaded the groceries into our car, I recounted my experience with Chris to my wife. After hearing the story, my wife suggested that Chris was "blog-worthy"—a term of reverence in our world.

I agreed. Chris was indeed *Teammate Tuesday* blog-worthy in the same way that good teammates like *Darnell the Mover (Teammate Tuesdays Volume I, Chapter 11), Amy the Balloon Lady (Teammate Tuesdays Volume I, Chapter 33)*, and *Caroline the Compassionate (Teammate Tuesdays Volume III, Chapter 38)* were. So I headed back into the grocery store to talk to Chris and snap a quick photo.

She graciously accepted my compliments but wanted to get her manager's permission before taking a photo. I thought: *Typical good teammate. Thinking of her team first.*

I followed Chris to her manager's office, expecting permission to be a mere formality. But that's not what happened. Chris knocked on the manager's door and peered into his office. I couldn't hear their conversation, but I could read her eyes well enough to know that something was amiss. Her smile faded.

A few moments later, the manager emerged from the office. He too was wearing a mask, only his eyes weren't smiling. His eyes communicated annoyance. I got the impression that I was inconveniencing him and he didn't appreciate the interruption. His first words to me were, "What is it that you want?"

I reiterated my praise of Chris and told him I'd like to write an article about her extraordinary service. Very bluntly, he told me that taking a photo would be against company policy. I was disappointed with his response but thanked him for his time and left the store.

I didn't feel the same way about this business when I left this time, however.

I expected to be writing a feature about quality customer service and how good teammates possess the ability to smile, even when they are wearing a mask. My interactions with Chris make for an inspiring good teammate anecdote. But my interactions with Chris' manager make for an important good teammate lesson: Good teammates accept compliments with gratitude and convey rejection with tact.

Chris's manager could have responded: "Ahh! Thank you so much. We think highly of Chris too. We're lucky to have her. I'm so sorry, but unfortunately our company policy doesn't allow photography without approval from our corporate headquarters. I appreciate your compliments and hope you understand." And he could have said it all with smiling eyes. Had he chosen that alternative approach, I most assuredly would have been more understanding.

I've deliberately omitted the name of the grocery store from this story. I continue to respect their business and don't plan to allow a negative interaction with one employee to taint my assessment. I've also deliberately included Chris's name in this story because a positive interaction with even one employee—who's a good teammate—should be recognized.

This story is a reminder of how impactful one individual can be on a team's reputation. The beauty is that we all get to choose which individual we want to be.

As always...Good teammates care. Good teammates share. Good teammates listen. Go be a good teammate.

Dive Donuts

JUNE 23

Many of my life's adventures have revolved around my affinity for savory BBQ and delicious donuts. I wrote about a "good teammate" lesson derived from an experience I had at a favorite BBQ spot in a previous blog ("Elle Lou's Secret," *Teammate Tuesdays Volume II*, Chapter 3). Today, it's the donut's turn.

Donuts are my guilty pleasure. I concede to their unhealthy nature, but I cannot resist the sweet deliciousness of fried dough.

I love Dunkin' Donuts. I love Voodoo Donuts. I love Duck Donuts. Seeing the orange "hot light" on in the window of a Krispy Kreme causes my heart to palpitate. Just thinking about the Fractured Prune (a delightful donut franchise in Ocean City, Maryland) makes my mouth water.

The latest edition to my list of favorite donuts is DG Donuts. The DG stands for "Damn Good"—and they most certainly are.

DG's donuts are enormous. They are thick and piled high with toppings. Holding them with one hand is hard to do. But what makes DG Donuts interesting is where they are sold.

A fellow donut aficionado turned me onto DG Donuts. He prefaced his recommendation with two suggestions: 1. Don't judge the donuts by where they are sold 2. Get there early in the morning because they tend to sell out.

DG Donuts are baked, decorated, and sold inside of a gas station along rural Highway 50 in Clermont, Florida. In fairness, the gas station is clean by gas station standards. But it is still a gas station.

DG Donuts are exactly why we shouldn't judge a book by its cover. What's inside and what comes out of the inside is what matters most. This truth also applies to good teammates.

Sometimes we focus on a person's shell and overlook the significance of what's inside of that person and how they use those skills to help their team. A good teammate's intangibles (e.g., attitude, enthusiasm, work ethic, integrity, tact, etc.) have a bigger impact on team success than we often realize.

A former basketball coach told me a story about an off-season experiment he conducted. He wanted to do something with his players other than the usual full court 5-on-5 games to determine who were his most valuable players. So he made his team play shorter, half court 3-on-3 games the entire off season. He changed the trios every day to keep his players from always playing on the same teams.

The coach kept track of wins and losses and then ranked his players individually by how many wins the teams they played on recorded. He expected his most talented and physically gifted players to have the most wins. However, that didn't turn out to be the case.

The players with the most wins lacked the physical stature and traditional benchmarks of those typically considered to be the team's best players. The players with the most wins were the ones everyone considered to be the team's best teammates. These players won more games because they made the other players around them better. Their intangibles amplified everyone else's talents.

Most team members focus on trivial details like their stats and their image. Good teammates concentrate on what matters most—the substance of their product. They focus on becoming a master of their role and utilizing their role to create success. And good teammates are *damn good* at creating success.

As always…Good teammates care. Good teammates share. Good teammates listen. Go be a good teammate.

Loyalty Blindness

JUNE 30

Do you like the ten-day "No Explanation Needed" challenges that pop up on Facebook? Surely, you've seen them. Respondents are supposed to post a different photo every day without providing any explanation for why they chose that photo. They then nominate someone else to do the same. Ten days. Ten photos. Ten nominations.

The challenges come in a variety of themes (e.g., best album covers, favorite books, vacation memories, pet photos, etc.). A lot of people love these posts. I, however, am not one of them.

Let me clarify: I love seeing the photos, but I hate their lack of context. I *require* an explanation. I want to know why that particular photo was chosen. The backstory interests me. To not receive an explanation is frustrating.

"No Explanation Needed" posts open themselves up to misinterpretation. Having to guess about the reasoning can create skewed conclusions.

When leaders try to operate in *no-explanation-needed* mode, they open themselves up to similar misunderstandings. They command without providing any explanation for why they want something done and expect blind obedience.

Good teammates are sometimes mistaken as being individuals who follow orders without question. But nothing could be further from the truth. Blind obedience is not a qualifying characteristic of good teammates.

Blind obedience leads to blind loyalty, which leads to *loyalty blindness*—the inability to recognize unethical and/or immoral behavior.

People become so loyal that they fail to see the pitfalls of their allegiance. Loyalty blindness facilitates cheating, corruption, and the tolerance of abusive behaviors. Good teammates don't allow themselves to get entangled in any of those compromising situations.

Leaders who demand blind obedience erroneously assume their approach compels compliance and efficiency. But demanding blind obedience enables dysfunction. Is there anything more inefficient than dysfunction?

Effective leaders provide context to their instructions. They want their team members to know the reasoning behind the decision. Their methodology provides transparency and builds mindful loyalty. Effective leaders are good teammates in that they value commitment over compliance.

Hall of Fame football coach Chuck Knoll had a favorite quote: "The mercenaries will always beat the draftees, but the volunteers will crush them both."

Draftees are motivated by fear. Mercenaries are motivated by money. Volunteers are motivated by purpose. Leaders who provide explanations clear the path for good teammates to pursue their purpose—serving the needs of their team.

Teams comprised of, and led by, good teammates (volunteers) achieve greater success.

As always...Good teammates care. Good teammates share. Good teammates listen. Go be a good teammate.*

The Addendum Teammate

JULY 7

I saw a mural painted on the wall of a resort that read "Just let go." It was a beach resort, so the message seemed appropriate. But the mural made me think about how adding an extra word can significantly alter a message's meaning. There's a difference between "Just let go" and "Just let it go."

"Just let go" is dropping your guard and ditching your convictions. Life is short. Eat the cake. Buy the shoes. Indulge in the simple pleasures. And so on.

"Just let it go" is abandoning emotions that are holding you back—like fear or anger. It's about adopting a "Frozen Mindset" (*Teammate Tuesday's Volume III,* Chapter 8) and not allowing yourself to be negatively influenced by what you cannot control.

I gave a talk to a group of sports officials a few years ago. One of the officials commented how hard it is to try to communicate to a coach who is complaining about the official not seeing something that happened. The official would attempt in earnest to tell the coach that he didn't see the play. I told the official that he needed to add an addendum to his reply.

Replying "Coach, I didn't see it" has the potential to escalate an already volatile situation. This response will lead the coach to question the official's competency or unfairly label the official as arrogant. The subsequent interactions won't likely be pleasant for either party.

To ward off that scenario, I suggested that the official should add the words *that way* to the end of his reply: "Coach, I didn't see it *that way*." This small addendum changes the message. The response is no longer susceptible to complaints of incompetency or arrogance. Now, the message is about different perspectives. Coaches have a much harder time arguing this reply.

Adding that small addendum allows the official to preserve his integrity without discounting the possibility that the coach may be right. The official conveys vulnerability by calmly acknowledging that interpretation is subjective to different vantage points. *What I saw from where I was standing isn't necessarily the same as what you saw.*

The altered response lets the coach know that the official is giving an honest effort and that the official is a person of principle. He isn't going to call something he doesn't see happening from his perspective.

Good teammates are principled people. They value integrity. Sometimes teams struggling to find the right chemistry need an *addendum teammate*—a teammate who compliments the team in a way that alters the team's culture for the better.

Addendum teammates don't necessarily need to be more physically or intellectually gifted to impact the team. Their contribution may be their lack of ego or their willingness to compromise. Adding an addendum teammate who is able to *just let go* and *just let it go* can unburden a team from what is holding it back.

If your team is struggling to jell as a unit, maybe you need the addition of an addendum teammate. Or maybe, you need to change your mindset and become your team's addendum teammate. One individual choosing to become a better teammate can change a team's entire culture.

As always…Good teammates care. Good teammates share. Good teammates listen. Go be a good teammate.

*(*By the way, sports officials—referees, umpires, etc.—are an essential component to the athletic experience. Plenty of "good teammates" occupy these positions. Be sure to thank them for their good-teammate-move presence!)*

Connecting Misfitted Teammates

JULY 14

Of all the unexpectedness that surfaced during the beginning of the COVID-19 pandemic, the shortage of jigsaw puzzles was among the most surprising. Shortages of toilet paper, disinfectant wipes, and hand sanitizer were arguably understandable. But who expected stores to sell out of jigsaw puzzles and for those shelves to remain empty for numerous weeks?

Working a puzzle entails an odd mix of elation and frustration. I suppose that's part of the appeal. Finding the four corner pieces provides a jolt of elation, as does completing the outside frame. Of course, the best elation comes from snapping the final puzzle piece into place.

But in between finding the four corners and snapping the final piece into place can lie a lot of frustration.

Scouring over a pile of puzzle pieces, searching for the right piece can be maddening—especially when you think you find the piece you were looking for and then discover it doesn't quite fit. No matter how hard you try, the piece just doesn't connect. If only there was a way for that piece to magically alter itself enough to properly fit.

Teams that struggle to come together often experience a similar problem when one of the team members doesn't seem to fit in with the rest of the team. They don't socialize or connect with the other members the way they could. Their not fitting in keeps the team from reaching its potential.

These individuals aren't necessarily bad people. They aren't misfits; they're *misfitted.* Maybe they're introverts and prefer solitude to their teammates' company. Or perhaps they favor a different approach to going about their business. Whatever the case may be, the bottom line is their way of conducting themselves is holding their team back.

While the frustration caused by this situation is similar to working a puzzle, it's not identical. Rigid puzzle pieces cannot alter themselves to properly fit. Misfitted team members can.

Fitting in requires the acceptance of inconvenience. Misfitted teammates may need to adjust their usual approach. They may need to become more aware of their habits that keep them from fitting in and consciously engage in opportunities to bond with their fellow teammates.

It should be noted that the other members of the team also bear a responsibility for solving the problem. The other team members must make a deliberate and consistent effort to include the misfitted teammate. This cannot be a some-of-the-time endeavor. It must be an all-of-the-time endeavor.

If team members are going to be hanging out or doing something together outside of the confines of normal team time, they should not only invite but insist that the misfitted teammate join them—even if that individual's presence makes them uneasy.

Altering a usual approach, increasing awareness, and consciously engaging in opportunities to bond with your fellow teammates may take you out of your comfort zone—and so may including teammates who might be difficult or make you uneasy. But the sacrifice of comfort is the price of team success.

To attain success, a team must get all of its pieces to connect and fit into place. Good teammates find a way to make this happen, regardless of whether they see themselves as a misfitted teammate or a member of the rest of the team.

As always…Good teammates care. Good teammates share. Good teammates listen. Go be a good teammate.

Seven Ways to Open Your New Team to Change

JULY 21

When someone joins an underperforming team, convincing the team's current members of the necessity for change can be a daunting task. Failing cultures are usually not, ironically, receptive to change. Their team members have grown accustomed to thinking that's the way we've always done it. Enticing them to embrace a new system and overcome their resistance requires a strategic approach.

Here are seven ways good teammates can ingratiate themselves and improve their chances of getting others to subscribe to the need for a change in culture:

1. **Respect history.** Your arrival may trigger a change in direction, but it doesn't mark the team's beginning. The team, even if underperforming, existed long before you arrived. Don't discount the team's history. Demonstrate respect by recognizing the past. I worked with a coach

who insisted on only wearing team apparel with vintage logos for the first six months after his hiring. The coach wanted to project respect by acknowledging his new team's roots and paying homage to them.

2. **Identify the positive.** A change in culture may be called for, but that doesn't mean everything your team was doing before you came on board is bad. Don't automatically throw the baby out with the bathwater. Be on the lookout for the positives. If you identify something your new team has been doing well, be sure to openly recognize and praise it. Praise will accentuate its importance and preserve its continuance.

3. **Ask before you suggest.** Adopt a personal policy of not suggesting a new strategy without first inquiring what other strategies have been tried in the past and the effectiveness of those strategies. Suggesting new strategies without inquiring about prior efforts will be interpreted as arrogant, insulting, and insensitive.

4. **Timing is everything.** Be extra cognizant of when you lobby for change. Suggesting a new method or criticizing an old method right before lunch may not be the best time. Expecting your teammates to process your suggestions while they're "hangry" probably won't lead to the results you desire. Neither will making a suggestion at five o'clock on a Friday or at opening bell on a Monday. Timing matters.

5. **Accelerate new traditions.** Traditions bind members to their team. Sometimes teams need to introduce new traditions to improve their culture. The problem, however, is establishing traditions takes time. Can you find a way to accelerate the process? Can you turn a popular annual event into a monthly or weekly event? Instead of recognizing a teammate of the year, can you celebrate a teammate of the month or week? Increased frequency leads to accelerated integration.

6. **Find a common adversary.** Few things generate unity quicker than a common enemy. Form an alliance with your new teammates through a mutual foe, even if you must manufacture a foe. I know of an administrator who would hire an outside consulting firm and instruct the consultants to deliberately make an unfavorable recommendation. The administrator would call the recommendation preposterous, side with her staff, and create unity. She united her team by aligning their contempt.

7. **Coach, don't coax.** You need to do more than make suggestions. Coaching entails explaining the reasons for your suggestions and a plan for implementation. Coaxing is merely promoting change and can be perceived as being manipulative. People are far more apt to invest in a different approach when they know why you want them to change.

To quote the legendary John Wooden: "Failure is not fatal, but failure to change might be." Good teammates recognize the value of change and embrace its unavoidable necessity—because doing so is what's best for their team.

As always...Good teammates care. Good teammates share. Good teammates listen. Go be a good teammate.

The Two-Way Mirror

JULY 28

A veteran gymnastics coach was eating dinner with his wife when he began to complain about his day. The coach loved what he did for a living and he loved his athletes. But he had grown increasingly frustrated by the way their parents were interfering with the training process.

Despite being a knowledgeable and accomplished instructor, who had been operating his own gymnastics academy for many years, the coach had reached a breaking point.

"The parents don't know what they're talking about," he told his wife. "They criticize the way I coach. They criticize the way I run the academy. They criticize the gymnasts' techniques. During competitions, they yell inaccurate instructions from the bleachers.

"Those parents undermine everything I'm trying to teach the kids and I've had enough of the divisiveness!"

The coach's wife interrupted him. "How do they know what you're trying to do?"

The coach initially interpreted his wife's question to be combative and lacking support. But the more he thought about her words, the more he recognized their legitimacy. She was right.

How were the parents supposed to know what he wanted? Training sessions were closed. The coach didn't want his gymnasts to be distracted, so he barred parents from entering the gym. He made them wait in the lobby, unable to observe what was being taught and emphasized.

The parents criticized his methodology because they lacked insight. They wanted their kids to experience success. Yelling instructions from the bleachers was their way of trying to help. By barring parents from training sessions, the coach had inadvertently created a void in understanding. The parents didn't know they were yelling inaccurate instructions.

The next morning, the coach cut a hole in the wall separating the lobby from the gym and installed a two-way mirror. The parents could now see how the coach was training their kids and what he was emphasizing, without distracting the athletes.

The two-way mirror changed everything. Parents became more supportive once they saw what the coach was doing with their own eyes. Being able to observe the training sessions gave them the insight they needed.

The parents began echoing the same encouragement to their kids as the coach. The two-way mirror got the parents on the same page as the coach. It also allowed the coach to start seeing the parents as assets instead of sources of hindrance.

My work affords me access to a lot of different sports teams and this access grants me a unique perspective in terms of how successful teams operate. The most successful teams—the ones who experience perennial success—include their athletes' parents in the process.

These teams allow their parents to observe their training sessions. Some of them have parents standing along the sidelines the entire practice. Others have parents peering into the training facility through large windows. I've even seen several elite academies livestream their training sessions and provide parents with login credentials.

Their transparency is the source of their success. The teams' transparency transforms the parents into team stakeholders and compels them to feel more like invested teammates than under-informed outsiders.

If your team is experiencing divisiveness, maybe it's time to take a look at your level of transparency. Investing in a two-way mirror could improve the depth of your stakeholders' investment.

As always…Good teammates care. Good teammates share. Good teammates listen. Go be a good teammate.

Choosing the Hard Right

AUGUST 4

I have been binge watching the legal drama *How to Get Away with Murder* on Netflix. In full disclosure (*pun intended), it is not the type of television show that normally appeals to me. I just sort of stumbled upon it and fell down the binge-watching rabbit hole.

If you're not familiar with the show, it revolves around a clever, yet often unscrupulous, defense attorney/law school professor named Annalise Keating (Viola Davis). Along with her team of ambitious subordinates—most of whom are current or former students—Keating attempts to navigate a web of ethical conundrums.

The show's ability to blur the lines between right and wrong is what drew me in. Its writers are gifted at crafting situations than compel viewers to sympathize with the characters' moral dilemmas and question the tolerable depth of loyalty.

How far would you go to conceal someone else's crime? What if the offender was someone you loved? What if the offender had an understandable reason for committing the crime? What if the offender had dirt on you? Could leverage coerce you into being complicit?

Every episode, despite the shows attempt to convey otherwise, I find myself consumed by the same thought: *These characters are not good teammates!*

The show tries to portray the characters as being loyal teammates, who are motivated by covering for each other's transgressions. Annalise and her cohorts keep secrets and commit crimes under the guise of protecting each other from harm. But their motives and actions aren't that pure.

They are motivated more by self-preservation than by a desire to protect others. When faced with moral crossroads, the characters never exhibit the courage to admit responsibility for their actions or the willingness to accept the consequences. They routinely choose the path of least resistance, regardless of whether that path is right or wrong.

Good teammates are guided by an old military adage: *Choose the hard right over the easy wrong.*

Choosing the hard right means selecting the option that is morally or ethically correct even if it's difficult. The easy wrong may provide you with initial relief, but the choice will inevitably lead to negative consequences. Whereas the hard right might initially involve unpleasant consequences, the choice will lead to inner peace.

Teammates who choose the hard right aren't ashamed of the face staring back at them in the mirror. They are free to function with an unburdened spirit. Teams comprised of clear-conscious teammates can overcome setbacks and focus on moving forward. The baggage of their past doesn't hold them back.

The storylines in *How to Get Away with Murder* ask viewers to accept the complexity of the characters' dilemmas. But their dilemmas aren't nearly as complex as they seem. The characters compound their problems by not applying the simple logic of choosing the hard right over the easy wrong.

How you respond to situations that test your integrity defines you as a teammate. Good teammates practice *mea culpa* (i.e. they acknowledge the fault in their actions) and always choose the hard right over the easy wrong.

As always…Good teammates care. Good teammates share. Good teammates listen. Go be a good teammate.

Ben Franklin's Filter

AUGUST 11

Conversing with people who have no "filter" can be brutal. They speak without tact, subtlety, or consideration. They seem to vocalize whatever thoughts pop into their heads, leaving us to wonder: Do they ever think about what they say before they say it?

Whenever they open their mouths, we cringe in anticipation of what's about to come out. Ironically, we're not offended by the brutality of their honesty; we're offended by the brutality of their insensitivity. Their lack of restraint creates an unpleasant atmosphere for everyone within earshot.

A favorite American Revolution story of mine involves a conversation between Ben Franklin and a younger, unpolished John Adams. During a gathering of the Continental Congress, Franklin votes in favor of a proposal, despite having privately divulged to Adams his strong opposition to the measure.

When the proposal is brought to the floor, Adams voices his disapproval, expecting Franklin to do the same. But Franklin says nothing.

Angered by the elder statesman's silence, Adams later confronts Franklin in a Philadelphia pub. He asks Franklin, "Do you not believe in saying what you think?" Franklin replies that he is quite against doing so, before famously declaring, "Thinking aloud is a habit which is responsible for most of mankind's misery."

Good teammates possess the discipline to refrain from thinking aloud. They have a filter, and they use it to minimize misery on their team. Their filter is a *drama-reducer*.

Drama enables dysfunction—an undisputed source of misery. Teams immersed in drama are too distracted to experience success. Their members are always fighting with each other, instead of fighting for each other.

Franklin believed movements are secured through diplomacy, which requires a degree of delicacy. Effective diplomats do not have the luxury of freely speaking their mind. They must constrain their thoughts and, occasionally, table their words.

Insensitive words can produce adverse outcomes, because insensitive words can be perceived as offensive words. Offensive words lead to defensive responses. Offended listeners are unlikely to be brought around to the speaker's way of thinking. Getting listeners to change their way of thinking is the diplomat's ultimate objective.

Similar to good diplomats, good teammates make it a habit to put themselves in a position to influence positive change. This requires them to choose their words wisely and vocalize their thoughts at opportune times and locations.

In a 1735 op-ed piece in *The Pennsylvania Gazette*, Ben Franklin advised Philadelphians to take precautions to prevent fires, a serious threat to colonial life. Franklin wrote: "An ounce of prevention is worth a pound of cure."

This nugget of wisdom also applies to team dynamics. Filtering our words is a way of preventing drama from destroying our teams. The inconvenience of prevention costs a lot less than the burden of reconstruction.

As always...Good teammates care. Good teammates share. Good teammates listen. Go be a good teammate.

Six Ways to Be a Good Virtual Teammate

AUGUST 18

A few months after my children's book *Be a Good Teammate* was published, I found myself standing at the end of my driveway waiting on the school bus to pick my daughters up for their first day of school. My daughters were insistent that I use my phone that morning to record a video of them before the bus came.

I wasn't sure what they wanted to film, but I didn't think it was a good time for them to play with my phone. I eventually caved, however, and I am glad I did. Their video captured a cute, unsolicited, unscripted, iconic moment in our lives. With complete sincerity, my daughters looked into the lens and, in unison, said: "First day of school and we're going to be good teammates this year."

If you're new to *Teammate Tuesdays*, you should know that I originally wrote *Be a Good Teammate* for my daughters—which made their video especially meaningful to me. Filming a *first-day-of-school-and-we're-going-to-be-good-teammates-this-year* video has become an annual tradition.

I share these videos on social media every year and often use them during my speeches. I think they are evidence of the influence the "good teammate" message can have when it is emphasized and nurtured.

My daughters went back to school this week, and keeping with tradition, we filmed another video. But this year's video had a different vibe. COVID-19 restrictions have delayed their return to brick-and-mortar classrooms. Like many other students, my daughters are starting the school year through distance learning.

In years past, I would ask my daughters when they got home from school if they made any good teammate moves that day. As I filmed their latest video, I wondered if my question would still be valid. How could they make good teammate moves without being at the school? After contemplating the issue, I have decided it is definitely possible. Here are six ways virtual students can be good teammates:

1. Treat your learning guide (parent, grandparent, older sibling, etc.) with the same respect that you would your brick-and-mortar teacher. The person monitoring your schoolwork deserves your gratitude and your respect. Be kind to them and don't cause them added stress.

2. Stay connected with your virtual teacher. Maintaining radio silence is not an acceptable communication

strategy. Respond promptly to your teacher's emails. The quicker you respond, the more appreciated it will be. Delayed replies lead to delayed learning.

3. Turn in your work by the required deadlines. Don't force your learning guide or your virtual teacher to hound you about missing assignments. Be considerate of their time by taking initiative and adhering to deadlines.

4. Use caution when handling/moving your device, avoid consuming food or drink near your device, and keep your device's battery charged or its AC cord plugged in. You can't learn from a disabled device. Carelessness could cause an unnecessary, and completely avoidable, interruption.

5. Be on the lookout for confused classmates. If a classmate or learning guide posts a comment about not understanding an assignment or being unable to find the assignment's instructions, share what you've discovered with them. You may be able to help them quicker than your teacher.

6. Give your teacher a "virtual" apple. Leaving an apple on a teacher's desk is a time-honored method for expressing gratitude. Distance learning can be as frustrating for your teacher as it is for you. Sending your teacher an e-card, a scanned copy of a drawing, or even a GIF letting them know you appreciate their efforts will be a treasured "good teammate move."

In case you haven't already realized, what is outlined above can also be applied to those forced to work virtually. I assure you, good bosses appreciate receiving "virtual" apples, too.

As always…Good teammates care. Good teammates share. Good teammates listen. Go be a good teammate.

*The first day of school videos referenced above can be viewed at https://www.coachloya.com/6-ways-to-be-a-good-virtual-teammate/

Lessons from a Crane

AUGUST 25

Florida is blessed with lots of interesting birds, many of which I had never encountered before I moved to the Sunshine state. The Sandhill Crane falls into this category.

I am not much of a birdwatcher. I tend to view birds the way Orson Welles viewed art ("I don't know anything about art, but I know what I like."). I like the Sandhill Crane.

Standing at about 48-inches tall, the Sandhill Crane is one of the biggest birds in North America. Its tall, skinny, knobby legs are attached to an oval-shaped feathery middle that tapers into a long slender neck. The bird's beak is nearly twice the length of its head.

Bigger birds are usually flightless, but Sandhill Cranes can fly. Seeing them fly is an unforgettable experience. Each flap of their massive wings makes a distinct thumping sound, accompanied by an even more distinct billowing caw. I imagine the experience to be similar to what it would have been like to have pterodactyls fly overhead.

Most of my encounters with Sandhill Cranes have occurred during walks through my neighborhood. Sandhill Cranes have moxie—a unique blend of determination, courage, and bravado. They are not easily frightened. If you happen upon one, don't expect it to step aside or fly away.

When Sandhill Cranes cross a street, they aren't bothered by onlookers or approaching traffic. A toot of the horn would clear most wildlife from the path, but not the Sandhill Cranes. They move at their own pace. I once saw a semi-tractor-trailer blow its horn at a group of Sandhill Cranes who refused to hurry across an intersection. The birds were unphased.

Crane-versus-vehicle standoffs offer applicable perspectives on both confidence and arrogance. How can someone not appreciate the confidence of a bird refusing to back down from a semi-tractor-trailer truck that could drive over the bird without even denting its bumper?

To be an effective teammate, you must exude confidence. Your confidence level is contagious and influences those around you. If you appear nervous, worried, or frightened, you validate your teammates' anxiety and give them permission to be nervous, worried, or frightened. Whereas if you project confidence, you calm their natural reactions to adversity. Your confidence injects others with hope.

While the Sandhill Cranes' behavior is admirable, it is also appalling. Their refusal to back down from the semi-tractor-trailer is laced with arrogance. The birds are either oblivious to how easily the truck could crush them, or they are taking advantage of the driver's kindness.

Whichever the case, Sandhill Cranes don't seem to mind inconveniencing others. By moving so leisurely and making traffic wait, they are sending the message that their time is more important than everyone else's—a mindset that is selfish and arrogant.

To be an effective teammate, you must never allow your confidence to encroach the borders of arrogance.

Arrogant teammates are disruptive. They polarize their teams. They're cavalier with risks. They overpower instead of empower. As much as confidence magnetizes, arrogance repulses.

Good teammates can project confidence without transmitting arrogance by being sincere and practicing intentional awareness. Acknowledge the danger, weigh the risks, and act accordingly with courage. Let your confidence stem from your genuine love for your team.

As always…Good teammates care. Good teammates share. Good teammates listen. Go be a good teammate.

At Least Your Mom Still Loves You

SEPTEMBER 1

A video periodically surfaces on social media of a little league baseball coach heading to the pitching mound to talk to his player, who has presumably not been pitching well. Viewers can't hear the actual audio of the coach, but a voiceover has been dubbed into the video from an onlooking dad guessing what the coach is saying.

The dad's guesses are offensive and completely inappropriate—and funny.

"If you don't start throwing strikes, there's going be an Amber Alert out for you before the end of this game."

"Well…you win some, and you lose some. Unless you're on the mound, then we lose them all."

"Do you always suck this bad, or is it just this special occasion today?"

"You better figure out when soccer tryouts are."

"No pressure, but if you don't strike this kid out, I'm going to fill your pockets with meatballs and throw you in a piranha pond."

"I know you're only twelve, but the high school coach just texted me and you're already cut."

The video is meant to be satirical. It has over eleven million views and seventy-four thousand reactions, the overwhelming majority of which are laughing tears emojis. I admit the video made me laugh. But it also made me cringe a because I know buried within the satire is an element of reality.

What player hasn't experienced a coach's sarcastic wrath? Some clichés exist because they are true. The sarcastic coach is one of them. While the coach's words may be funny to those on the periphery, they are rarely enjoyable to their target.

I'm not trying to take anything away from the comedic nature of the video. I get that it is satire. But I think the video is so over-the-top that it makes for a good opportunity to remind coaches of the significance of the words they choose.

A coach's words are like tattoos on a player's soul. Be careful because even removed tattoos leave scars.

Sometimes apologies, subsequent praise, and the passing of time are not enough to erase the damage caused by hurtful words. This is a reminder that applies to not only coaches, but also to parents, teachers, bosses, or anyone in a position of authority.

One of the great ironies in sports is that coaches at the lowest levels receive the least amount of training yet possess the greatest amount of influence over their players' lives. The lower the level, the more cautious the coach must be. Innocent sarcasm can result in unintended, lasting harm to the emotionally undeveloped.

The aforementioned video ends with the coach telling his dejected player, "Well, at least your mom still loves you." Although it's the final clip in the video, it's my favorite.

Knowing that despite your shortcomings someone still loves you is comforting. This is the advantage of having good teammates on your side. No matter how poorly you play or how badly you mess up, they still love you. The unwavering support of a good teammate can inspire you to bounce back and strive to be a better version of yourself.

If you are a teammate in a position of influence, consider bypassing the sarcasm in favor of encouragement. No varsity coach will ever cut you for making that choice.

As always…Good teammates care. Good teammates share. Good teammates listen. Go be a good teammate.

**The video of the baseball coach speaking to his little pitchers can be found at https://www.facebook.com/watch/?v=315312109222436*

Both Hands In

SEPTEMBER 8

Yogi Berra was one of baseball's most memorable characters. The Hall of Fame catcher was a three-time MVP, won ten World Series rings as a player, and another three as a manager. His baseball accomplishments were framed by his folksy personality and his witty quotes—aptly referred to as *Yogi-isms.*

> *"The future ain't what it used to be."*
> *"It's deja vu all over again."*
> *"You can observe a lot by watching."*
> *"Nobody goes there anymore. It's too crowded."*

I love yogi-isms. They are a combination of mixed metaphors, malapropisms, clever observations, and oddly insightful advice.

Archie Bunker was one of television's most memorable characters. The *All in the Family* patriarch also had a knack for dispensing notable one-liners—aptly referred to as *Bunker-isms.*

> *"We better not kill our chickens before they cross the road."*
> *"If it's too hot in the kitchen, stay away from the cook."*
> *"We're just sweeping dirty dishes under the rug."*

My youngest daughter and I were recently having a conversation about the importance of being fully committed to goals when she provided a *Yogi-ism*-meets-*Bunker-ism* response: "Dad, I've got two hands in, and they're not coming out."

She did to dipping your toe in the water, having one foot out the door, and having both feet in what Archie Bunker did to *Why did the chicken cross the road?* and *Don't count your chickens until they hatch.*

I understood what my daughter meant, and quite frankly, I think her response is a more accurate depiction of a good teammate's commitment level.

Having two feet in is supposed to illustrate commitment. But it's not always that simple. Some team members mistake practicing compliance as being committed. In other words, they follow policies, toe the line, don't rock the boat, and generally adhere to all the other expected clichés.

Anybody can live up to the standards of compliance by merely standing with two feet in. Good teammates, however, do more than practice compliance. They're proactive, which makes my daughter's *having-two-hands-in* analogy a more accurate depiction.

Hands imply activity. Good teammates are willing to *get their hands dirty, take matters into their own hands,* and be *hands on.* Hard workers use their hands, and so do good teammates.

What I most like about my daughter's response is the last part about her hands not coming out. Isn't that what being fully committed entails? Once you commit to something, you refuse to quit. You remain steadfast in your efforts until the objective is accomplished.

Successful teams are comprised of teammates who put two hands in and refuse to take them out, because—as Yogi Berra would say—*It ain't over 'til it's over.*

As always…Good teammates care. Good teammates share. Good teammates listen. Go be a good teammate.

Reality Is Everything

SEPTEMBER 15

Perception is everything. Or is it? You can dress in nice clothes, style your hair, wear fancy jewelry, or drive a sports car. But if your bank account reads zeros, the reality is you're broke.

The same reality applies to being a good teammate. You can look the part and say all the right things. But if deep down in your heart, you are jealous, have selfish motives, or lack understanding, you're not a good teammate. You're broken.

Last week, we debuted a new quiz on our website that rates "good teammate" strengths. I am blown away by how many people have already taken this quiz!

The most common feedback I've heard so far was that "the quiz really made (people) think" about what kind of teammate they are. Many also noted that they were surprised by how low they scored on parts of the quiz. I was not surprised by either of these responses.

The quiz was specifically designed to make people think about what kind of teammate they are. Most people don't spend a lot of time pondering this topic. Most people rely on their gut instincts to fill in the parameters.

I envisioned coaches, bosses, and team leaders having their entire teams take the quiz. The questions are generalized and therefore applicable to sports teams, corporate teams, school faculties, church teams, families, etc. Any team can gain insight by taking the free quiz. The results are intended to provide support to leaders wishing to broach the subject of being better teammates with their team members.

Because most people don't devote a lot of time thinking about what kind of teammate they are, they tend to overestimate their own abilities—a product of a psychological phenomenon known as the Dunning–Kruger effect.

For example, several people who took the quiz commented that they were surprised they scored low in the category of loyalty, since they generally consider themselves to be a loyal person. (FYI, the quiz measures aptitude in five different categories: Active, Loyal, Invested, Viral, and Empathetic.) By all traditional benchmarks, they probably are loyal. But good teammates view loyalty through a slightly different lens.

Most people think of loyalty as being a two-way street. They are loyal to entities that are loyal to them. (i.e. If you get my back, I'll get yours.) Good teammates, however, are loyal to what they believe in, regardless of what they get in exchange for their efforts. Good teammates are motivated by commitment, not reciprocated benefits (i.e. I've got your back. Whether you've got mine or not, I've got yours.)

That mentality leads to a team-first culture and allows teams to withstand challenging times. Relationships are based on commitment instead of the fragility of bartering. When the concept of loyalty is framed in this manner, those who were surprised to have scored low in the category begin to realize the potential flaw in their previous way of thinking.

It is important to point out that just because individuals score low on a part of the quiz doesn't necessarily mean that they are bad people. The low score should be taken as an indication that maybe those individuals need to reexamine how they view the subject and the depth of their understanding.

They shouldn't be discouraged; they should be encouraged, because they discovered an area in which they can focus on improving upon. Good teammates are always on the lookout for ways to get better. Providing opportunities to get better is how effective leaders heal broken teammates.

As always...Good teammates care. Good teammates share. Good teammates listen. Go be a good teammate.

Voluntold Teammates

SEPTEMBER 22

I overheard a conversation the other day that made me think about an issue that plagues underperforming teams yet is irrelevant to teams comprised of good teammates. The man standing next to me was telling his friend how he had spent the entire day cleaning out his company's supply room. I didn't get the impression that this was an especially enjoyable task for him.

With an unenviable look, his friend asked, "Did you volunteer for that job?"

"No. They couldn't get anybody else to do it, so I was sort of volunteered," the man replied.

His friend shot back, "Oh, you mean you were voluntold."

Voluntold. Isn't that the perfect way to describe situations where individuals are forcibly assigned an unpleasant task? Once common military slang, the term has now worked its way into pop vernacular. Being *volunteered* is laced with irony. Being *voluntold* is laced with accuracy.

A person who is voluntold is told what to do. Declining isn't an option, which attaches a negative undertone to the concept. Nobody wants to be told they have to do an unpleasant task.

From a leadership perspective, no quality leader wants to have to tell someone to do an unpleasant task. When leaders are left with no other recourse but to forcibly assign an unpleasant task, they risk being resented, creating disgruntled workers, and having to deal with what will likely be subpar results. All of which contribute to a toxic culture.

Teams that rely on work getting done by members who've been voluntold are doomed to underachieve, because the members' hearts will never truly be into their work. Teams made up of good teammates, on the other hand, don't have this problem.

Good teammates embrace opportunities to volunteer for anything that could potentially help their team be more successful. They don't necessarily enjoy doing unpleasant tasks any more than anyone else. But they are willing to engage in unpleasant work that is beneficial to their team's core mission—without hesitation. Good teammates don't have to be voluntold.

This reality is one of the many reasons that quality leaders appreciate and value good teammates, and why teams with good teammates accomplish more.

The mercenaries beat the draftees because they have a greater source of motivation. Volunteers crush draftees and mercenaries because they also have a greater source of motivation—a commitment to serve the needs of their team.

Consistent commitment defines a good teammate, and that commitment is fueled by passion. Passion can override anxiety, fear, repugnance, and apprehension. Passion can turn the daunting into the delighted.

The next time you are voluntold for a task, consider why you had to be. Perhaps your commitment to your team isn't as strong as it should be and it's time to increase your passion.

As always...Good teammates care. Good teammates share. Good teammates listen. Go be a good teammate.

Follow Roles

SEPTEMBER 29

When I was in second grade, we did a fun assignment in Mrs. Duppstadt's class that required us to design our own restaurant. We had to come up with everything from what the restaurant would be called to what food would be served to how our employees would be dressed. It was a marvelous assignment for fostering creative thinking.

School wasn't always an enjoyable experience for me as a kid. But I remember being completely engrossed in this assignment and having so much fun designing my restaurant—2L's Food Lounge.

My mother recently downsized to a new house and sent me a box of "things" from my childhood that she had kept over the years. Included in the box was a folder with my second-grade restaurant assignment. I don't know why she kept it, but I'm glad she did. What a blast from the past!

As I leafed through the pages, I realized that Mrs. Duppstadt's assignment was essentially a business plan. We had to draw pictures of what we envisioned the exterior of our building would look like. We had to provide a floor plan for its interior. We had to list our menu prices. We even had to provide the "secret recipe" for our house specialty, which at 2L's Food Lounge was going to be a quarter pound hamburger on a poppyseed bun topped with an American flag. (I have no idea why I chose that combination!)

Revisiting Mrs. Duppstadt's assignment brought about two revelations: First, I wasn't nearly as creative nor original as I remembered myself being. Second, I was an atrocious speller! However, in at least one instance, my wayward spelling produced an unintentional yet profoundly accurate statement.

An activity in the assignment asked us to list qualifications for personnel we intended to hire to work in our restaurant. In my elementary school scrawl, I listed: clean, smart, and follow roles.

In a way, the qualification I listed conveyed my desire to hire people who were good teammates. Good teammates practice cleanliness. It's a way of conveying pride and consideration for others. They are also competent—a synonym of smart. A spelling mistake with the last qualification, though, offers an insightful perspective.

I suspect the second-grade version of me meant to write "follow rules" instead of "follow roles." The current version of me thinks the spelling gaffe to be more pertinent. An adherence to roles is more significant than an adherence to rules. While good teammates respect compliance (following rules), they are more concerned with their commitment to their role.

Teammates who follow roles enable teams to operate with synergy. They make the whole greater than the sum of its parts. Appreciating the importance of roles is what ultimately defines the components of a team. Good teammates understand that every role on the team matters and that their teams' maximum achievement is dependent upon every member mastering his or her role.

You can occasionally get away with disregarding rules, but no team succeeds with its members disregarding roles.

A final revelation worth sharing: The restaurant assignment reminded me that Mrs. Duppstadt was a wonderful teacher and a good teammate to many. May her example and her willingness to empower others inspire you to do the same.

As always…Good teammates care. Good teammates share. Good teammates listen. Go be a good teammate.

When Teammates Are Smart

OCTOBER 6

Every morning before begrudgingly heading off to work in the sweltering open hearths of Bethlehem Steel, Pete Carril's father offered his son the same advice: *The strong always take from the weak, but the smart take from the strong. Choose to be smart.*

The younger Carril would grow up to be the legendary Princeton basketball coach. His father's advice would became the driving theme to his innovative coaching philosophies and the eventual title to his 1997 memoir: *The Smart Take from the Strong.*

In the last chapter, I wrote that good teammates are smart. I've been thinking about that assessment in relationship to Carril's words. What specifically do good teammates do that make them smart? What separates them from the strong and the weak? What is the difference between being intelligent and being smart?

Intelligence stems from our genetic makeup. We are, theoretically, born with this ability to acquire knowledge. Smart is the ability to apply the knowledge we acquire. In terms of team dynamics, smart is a far more useful characteristic. Intelligence is meaningless without application.

Understanding the difference between smart and intelligent allows us to understand what specifically makes a teammate smart:

- Their work ethic
- Their commitment to continuous learning
- Their capacity to take calculated risks

The smart know the value of hard work. They recognize that hard work isn't just intrinsically virtuous, but that it increases the probability of positive outcomes. When people work toward a goal, they improve the chances of their achieving that goal. The harder they work, the greater the probability. Good teammates have work ethic and a readiness to outwork others.

The smart are committed to continuous learning. They constantly seek new and better ways to operate. They anticipate change and develop improved training methods. Good teammates master their craft by avoiding repeated mistakes and the pitfalls of complacency.

The smart advance themselves through calculated risks. Failure to adapt can be fatal, but so can failure to consider the consequences of our actions. Good teammates strike the right balance of confidence and caution by weighing the risks before they act and by not allowing themselves to be paralyzed by the presence of risk.

Laziness precludes the weak from outworking others or committing to lifelong learning. Risk renders the weak unable to venture from their comfort zones. The weak are not good teammates because they mentally defeat themselves.

Though capable of hard work, arrogance keeps the strong from embracing the need to evolve. The strong are too content to rely on the comfort provided by their strength to self-evaluate, which can cause them to be cavalier in the risks they take. They also mentally defeat themselves.

It's important to note that the strong can be smart, and so can the intelligent. Being smart is a choice, and so is being a good teammate.

As always…Good teammates care. Good teammates share. Good teammates listen. Go be a good teammate.

Ten Habits of Good Teammates

OCTOBER 13

For better or worse, we are defined by our habits. What we consistently do sets the boundaries of our comfort zone. Since we tend to function at the mean of our comfort zone, our habits play a crucial part in determining the extent of our success. Successful people have habits that facilitate their success. Good teammates have habits that facilitate their teams' success.

Here are ten habits of good teammates:

1. **They Respect Time**

Time is everyone's most cherished commodity. Good teammates value their time and that of others by practicing efficiency, keeping on schedule, and refusing to be late. And they hold their teammates accountable to the same standards.

2. **They Adjust Their Mood**

Individuals who "wear their emotions on their sleeve" make for poor teammates. Good teammates adjust their mood to meet the needs of their team. If the team is flat, they project energy. If the team is despondent, they project hope. If the team is overzealous, they project restraint.

3. **They Speak with Tact**

Situations occasionally emerge where we are called to confront behaviors that threaten our team's culture. While it may be tempting to convey disapproval with brutality, good teammates confront with tact. They speak their demands without being demeaning.

4. **They Empathize Before They Criticize**

Passing judgment without first considering possible mitigating circumstances can lead to resentment and misunderstandings—which fracture teams. Good teammates consider issues from alternative viewpoints before they criticize offenders.

5. **They Seek Opportunities to Learn**

When it comes to knowledge, good teammates are not content with the status quo. They are lifelong learners who continuously seek opportunities to increase their knowledge. Becoming more knowledgeable puts them in a better position to help their team grow.

6. They Solicit Self-Assessment

Related to the previous point, good teammates want to become better versions of themselves. They realize others may not always be able or willing to provide them with adequate feedback, so they proactively self-assess. They have the humility to routinely ask themselves: *What can I do better?*

7. They Engage in Self-Care

Mental, emotional, and physical health affect our capacity to serve. Good teammates engage in self-care by eating properly, exercising regularly, and getting sufficient rest. They take care of themselves, so they are able to care of others.

8. They Stay Connected

Good teammates make a conscious effort to maintain connections with the other members of their team, even if doing so requires them to be inconvenienced. When they can't connect through in-person interactions, they utilize phone calls, text messages, emails, handwritten notes, and social media.

9. They Listen with Intent

We learn through listening, not speaking. Good teammates are intentional listeners in that they listen with the purpose of discovering the speakers' thoughts. Good teammates don't interrupt others and they don't think about their response while others are speaking. They focus on what is being said and why it is being said.

10. **They Grasp the Influence of Their Example**
Our example is everything! Humans are wired to look to others for behavioral guidance. Mirror neurons cause us to mimic the words and actions of those with whom we surround ourselves. Good teammates demonstrate their awareness of this situation in every decision they make.

Bad habits can confine us. Good habits can refine us. If you want to define yourself as a good teammate, you must develop good habits.

As always…Good teammates care. Good teammates share. Good teammates listen. Go be a good teammate.

Grouchy Teammates

OCTOBER 20

Fifty-one years ago last week, Oscar the Grouch made his debut on *Sesame Street.* To commemorate the event, the fifteenth day of October is now recognized as National Grouch Day—a date for all grouches to celebrate their way of life.

According to the holiday's website, a grouch is "an eccentric creature that loves to complain and is happiest when someone can share their misery." Grouches are cantankerous malcontents. Sound redundant? It was meant to be.

I posted a photo of Oscar the Grouch on my social media pages on Thursday, accompanied by the following text: *Today's #NationalGrouchDay! (Remember: Good teammates are never grouchy…don't give in!)*

I thought the post to be apropos. Someone later messaged me that "Everybody feels grouchy now and then."

I am not a fan of "Everybody…" assessments, like *Everybody* has flaws or *Everybody* has fears or *Everybody* has skeletons in their closet. Those sorts of extreme statements usually have exceptions. And though sometimes intended to provide solace, they are more often than not used as justification for unacceptable behavior. In this instance, however, I concede that everybody does occasionally feel grouchy.

When Oscar the Grouch made his *Sesame Street* debut, he was orange instead of green. His first on-camera words were: "Don't bang on my can." He then proceeded to unleash a slew of unpleasantries on his human visitors before rudely declaring: "Close my can, would you? You're letting all the fresh air and sunlight in. Boy, I hate that."

Oscar the Grouch's surly disposition is markedly different than that of his *Sesame Street* neighbor, Big Bird. Their personalities are practically polar opposites. Big Bird is kind, friendly, and welcoming. He is inquisitive and takes an interest in others' lives. He makes friends easily.

Surprisingly, Big Bird's first on-camera words were not that much different than Oscar's. When Big Bird first comes on the screen, he crashes into an alley door and complains, "Silly door. Always in my way."

His demeanor immediately changes when he sees Gordon and Sally—the same humans who tried to interact with Oscar—standing in the street. Big Bird conquers his unhappy feelings and greets his guests with enthusiasm. He prioritizes their need to be greeted over his negative response to crashing into the door.

Feeling grouchy and acting grouchy are two different entities. How we respond to our grouchy feelings shapes our relationships. Good teammates set their grouchiness aside for the betterment of their team. They project the emotions their team needs over their instinctive reactions.

Interestingly, and also ironically, the late Caroll Spinney provided the voice and puppeteering for both Big Bird and Oscar the Grouch. Perhaps his presence in both characters is symbolic of our option to choose the type of teammate we want to be.

We can choose selfishness and be like Oscar the Grouch. Or, we can choose selflessness and be like Big Bird.

As always...Good teammates care. Good teammates share. Good teammates listen. Go be a good teammate.

**Details about National Grouch day are from https://nationaltoday.com/national-grouch-day/. Details about Sesame Street and Carroll Spinney are from https://muppet.fandom.com/wiki/Caroll_Spinney*

How to Handle Ghost Teammates

OCTOBER 27

Is your team haunted by ghost teammates? Halloween is the perfect occasion to discuss the menacing nature of ghost teammates—team members who disappear when they are needed the most.

Ghost teammates are not dependable. They have an aversion to challenges and a knack for vanishing anytime they might be inconvenienced.

Ghost teammates are fence-riders, space-fillers, and work-avoiders. They don't take initiative. They don't take responsibility. And they don't ever take a stand. The only commitment they take seriously is their commitment to remain as invisible as possible. Too many ghost teammates will haunt your team.

Fortunately, eliminating ghost teammates doesn't necessitate a séance, exorcism, or any other type of supernatural intervention. The solution is usually just a matter of getting them to realize the impact their *ghostly* behaviors have on the rest of their team.

Make sure ghost teammates know that you see them. Consider the ghosts from the movie *Beetlejuice*, Adam (Alec Baldwin) and Barbara (Geena Davis). Once they realized that Lydia (Wynona Ryder) could see them, their approach changed. They became much more mindful of their actions.

The same is true for ghost teammates. They require paranormal attention. Acknowledgement draws them out of the shadows. Deliberately recognize ghost teammates during team gatherings beyond the scope of what you normally would. Motivate them to be more invested in the team by putting them on the spot and not allowing them to remain invisible.

Team success is dependent upon every team member making meaningful contributions. Allowing some members to get away with not pulling their weight will lead to resentment, and it won't be long until dysfunction creeps into the team's culture.

To ward off resentment, you must "unmask" ghost teammates. Think about the gang from *Scooby Doo* unmasking the old miner's ghost. (I would've gotten away with it if it wasn't for you meddling kids!) The old miner's ghost had everyone, including himself, fooled until the gang took off his mask and exposed his true identity. He got away with "it," until he couldn't.

Lay out expectations and hold team members accountable to those expectations. Let ghost teammates know that you see them for what they are, others see them for what they are, and that they need to see themselves for what they are—a detriment to their team's culture. This tactic will increase their self-awareness and minimize their anonymity.

Ghost teammates may not be dead, but they are certainly not A.L.I.V.E. (Active, Loyal, Invested, Viral, and Empathetic—the five key good teammate behaviors). Until your team is purged of ghost teammates, it will continue to be terrorized by their presence.

As always...Good teammates care. Good teammates share. Good teammates listen. Go be a good teammate.

The Beauty of Seasoned Teammates

NOVEMBER 3

I love the beauty of fall foliage. Mother Nature always seems to pick the perfect combination of colors. She chooses just the right amount of reds, yellows, and oranges to paint a foliage masterpiece.

Unfortunately, I don't get to experience the changing of the leaves where I live in Florida the way I did growing up in Pennsylvania. Palm trees generally stay the same color throughout year. Don't get me wrong, I love palm trees and a lot of other aspects of living in Florida. But this time of year, I miss the colors of the leaves.

As a boy, I enjoyed running and jumping into piles of raked leaves. As a teenager, I enjoyed earning money raking leaves for my grandmother. As an adult, I loathed raking leaves, but I enjoyed watching my daughters play in them. I also enjoyed the colorful backdrop the leaves provided for all of those memories.

Humans tend to not appreciate the beauty of an experience until it becomes a memory. The key to maximizing life is to cherish the beauty of the moment while you're living it. This philosophy applies to being a good teammate.

Like the leaves, teams change every season. No two teams are ever the same. The addition of new members and the departure of others alters team dynamics. Responsibilities change. Roles evolve. Yet standards remain.

How effectively team members embrace the change without abandoning standards will determine the new team's success.

One of the hardest obstacles to overcome during this transitional period is replacing the loss of the team's most experienced members. Good teammates realize change is inevitable and appreciate the limited amount of time they have to tap into the wisdom of their seasoned teammates—while those individuals are still part of the team. Good teammates accomplish this through four steps:

1. **They ask questions.** Lots of questions! As time passes, people forget. Seasoned teammates are no exception, which is why good teammates ask them detailed questions about procedures, techniques, and operations before that knowledge fades.

2. **They prod seasoned teammates to tell stories.** Sometimes we don't know what we don't know—or need to know. We aren't able to ask questions about

topics of which we are unaware. Prodding seasoned teammates to tell stories about their time on the team can be enlightening, especially in regards to team history.

3. **They shut up, sit back, listen, and absorb.** We learn through listening, not speaking. When seasoned teammates speak, good teammates become intentional listeners. They don't compromise the opportunity by allowing their mind to wander or by thinking about what they want to say next. They absorb what the seasoned teammates are saying.

4. **They document what they learned.** Good teammates understand that their memories are also susceptible to fading as time passes, so they document what they learn from seasoned teammates. Preserved wisdom leads to perpetuated success.

The beauty of fall foliage only lasts for a brief period, as does that of seasoned teammates. Tap into their knowledge. Capture their wisdom. But most importantly, cherish their presence.

As always...Good teammates care. Good teammates share. Good teammates listen. Go be a good teammate.

Preventing Teammates from Bad Juju

NOVEMBER 10

Even though my blog is about teammates and teamwork, I don't usually include content about specific sports teams or current sporting events. I try to steer clear of that type of content because I don't want the value of *Teammate Tuesdays* compromised by what could be perceived as me being partial to one team or another.

But I'm going to break protocol this week and discuss an incident that happened during Sunday's Dallas Cowboys versus Pittsburgh Steelers game at AT&T Stadium because the incident so perfectly illustrates an important good teammate trait.

With the Steelers trailing the Cowboys late in the second half, Steelers' wide receiver JuJu Smith-Schuster caught a thirty-yard touchdown pass to get his team back into the game. The play changed the game's momentum.

Smith-Schuster is known for his creative end zone celebrations. They send his two million TikTok followers (including both of my daughters) into a frenzy. But instead of launching into a spirited dance or mimed antics after this touchdown, Smith-Schuster uncharacteristically got up and began carrying the ball back toward the line of scrimmage, void of any apparent fanfare.

When asked about the lack of celebration in a post-game interview, Smith-Schuster revealed that he had intended to take the ball to the center of the field and dance on the Dallas Cowboys' logo—an act the host team considers to be taboo and blatantly disrespectful.

In September 2000, the Forty Niners' Terrell Owens famously celebrated on the Cowboys' midfield logo after scoring a touchdown. He was pummeled by Dallas defender George Teague shortly thereafter. The confrontation resulted in ejections and suspensions on both teams.

As Smith-Schuster jogged in the direction of midfield on Sunday, the Cowboys' Antwaun Woods stalked him, anticipating that the Steeler's receiver may attempt to replicate Owens' notorious celebration. Woods appeared ready to pounce should that be the situation. That's when Smith-Schuster's teammate, James Conner, intervened.

Smith-Schuster told reporters after the game that Conner came over and reminded him that it was still a close game and that celebrating on the logo would not be a good idea. (*Good teammate move* by James Conner!)

Good teammates keep us from making mistakes that we will later regret. They intervene before we act irresponsibly, irrationally, or irreversibly. They prevent problems by saving us from ourselves.

Had JuJu Smith-Schuster carried through with his plan, what ensued would have most certainly resulted in—if you'll pardon the pun—*bad juju* for JuJu Smith-Schuster, and his team. Dallas would have felt disrespected and retaliated. Pittsburgh would have then felt obligated to come to their player's aid.

Smith-Schuster's celebration could have led to penalties that cost his team the game. Or worse, it could have gotten someone seriously—and unnecessarily—injured.

While Conner's intervention is notable, it's only half of the good teammate lesson to be learned from this incident. The other half, ironically, comes from Smith-Schuster. When a trusted teammate recommends foregoing potentially doomful action, good teammates have the humility to trust the recommendation.

Smith-Schuster chose to trust James Conner. He set his ego aside, listened to what Conner had to say, and acquiesced. His trust and humility are commendable good teammate traits that often go unrecognized. But they too are worthy of acknowledgement.

As always...Good teammates care. Good teammates share. Good teammates listen. Go be a good teammate.

Assessing Through Confident Humility

NOVEMBER 17

In September, we launched a new Good Teammate Assessment Quiz on our website. Over the last two and half months, tens of thousands of people from fifrty states and thirty-one countries have taken the quiz. The response has been unbelievable!

One comment that we keep hearing from people who've taken the quiz is that they scored lower than they expected. I am not surprised by that feedback, as I expected that to be the case.

Most people overestimate their "good teammate" abilities. They think they are better teammates than they are, especially when their self-assessment lacks context.

By nature, we tend to measure ourselves by the relativity of our surroundings. When compared to the selfish people on our under-performing team, our behavior can seem exceptional. But when compared to the selfless people on exceptional teams—true good teammates—our behavior can fall short of the mark.

Take for instance the category of loyalty. Of the six categories assessed in the good teammate quiz, the loyalty scores have consistently been the lowest. I suspect the reason for this to be the product of ignorance, as opposed to arrogance.

Most people want to be good teammates and consider themselves to be loyal. Though when pushed, they frequently reveal that their loyalty is contingent upon others being loyal to them. Their loyalty is bartered. (i.e. If you're loyal to me, I'll be loyal to you.)

Good teammates don't operate that way. Good teammates are loyal to their team and their fellow teammates regardless of what they get in exchange for their loyalty. To them, loyalty is an unwavering commitment to the team's ideology and is contingent solely upon their belief in its ideology. This philosophy is why good teammates are able to humble themselves to serve the needs of their team.

Many of the people who scored lower than they expected on the quiz described their reactions as moving through three stages: defense, acceptance, and reflection.

At first, they doubted the validity of the assessment. They became defensive and tried to refute the results. But then they calmed down and accepted their score. They realized that they answered the questions honestly, so the results were probably accurate.

After they accepted the results, they began to reflect on their answers. They acknowledged that maybe they aren't as good of a teammate as they thought they were and that they have some behaviors they should try to improve upon.

Their ability to arrive at a point of reflection where they are willing to consider their need for improvement speaks more to their character than their score on the quiz. Their receptiveness to the possibility of being deficient shows humility. And confident humility leads to growth.

The good teammate quiz is an effective method of getting team members to see themselves through a different lens. The quiz gives leaders an opportunity to discuss deficiencies with individuals who need to be better teammates.

Around the same time that we launched the good teammate quiz, we also launched an online video course designed to help teams improve teamwork. The response to the course has been equally unbelievable.

Leaders who've had their teams complete the course have raved about the impact it had on their team's culture. Both the quiz and the course are intended to get individuals to think about 1) what sort of teammate they are, 2) what does it mean to be a good teammate on their team, and 3) what do they need to do to be a better teammate.

A desire to discover answers to those three questions sets the wheels of team success in motion.

As always…Good teammates care. Good teammates share. Good teammates listen. Go be a good teammate.

When Thanks Isn't Enough

NOVEMBER 24

Thanksgiving is my favorite holiday, bar none. Some of my fondest memories come from celebrating Thanksgiving at my grandmother's house. The holiday includes all my favorites—food, family, fun, and football. For me, it doesn't get much better than that.

Thanksgiving is supposed to be a time to reflect on your blessings. You'll hear the cliché "attitude of gratitude" tossed around a lot over the next few days, and you'll likely find yourself pondering at some point what you are thankful for in your life. Those thoughts will undoubtedly envelop you in a warm, pleasant feeling of content.

But what about what you are not thankful for? What about the parts of your life that are keeping you from being the best version of yourself? What about the parts of your life that are keeping you from experiencing true happiness? Maybe it's a job you hate, or a relationship that soured, or bad habit you have yet to shed.

An attitude of gratitude can ward off negativity. But an attitude of gratitude can also be a cage that confines you to the status quo. It can enable contentment that causes you to endure when you should be modifying.

In his book *What Happy People Know*, Dr. Dan Baker writes: "the threatening messages from your amygdala [fear center of the brain] and the anxious instincts of your brainstem are cut off, suddenly and surely, from access to your brain's neocortex…It is a fact of neurology that the brain cannot be in a state of appreciation and a state of fear at the same time."

In other words, humans can't feel stressed and grateful at the same time. It's not physiologically possible. For that reason, I understand why focusing on gratitude could be beneficial to a person's psyche. Who wants to feel stressed? However, the parts of our life that stress us are usually the parts that need addressed, and not suppressed.

When you're listing what you're thankful for this week, be sure to include having the opportunity to change what you're not thankful for.

I believe in the power of positivity and have, on many occasions, touted the influence that "but-statements" can have on attitude. (I hate getting up early, but I'm thankful I have a job. I don't like cleaning my house, but I am thankful I have a roof over my head.)

I'm also generally a thankful person, yet the biggest and best changes in my life have come from my not being thankful. Sometimes, the most important but-statement you can make is: I might have to temporarily put up with this, but I'm not going to accept it.

May you have a happy Thanksgiving. Eat lots of turkey. Laugh with your family. And allow yourself to be grateful for the opportunity to change the parts of your life for which you are not thankful.

As always…Good teammates care. Good teammates share. Good teammates listen. Go be a good teammate.

The Gift of Talent

DECEMBER 1

The fact that the release of my weekly blog always falls on #GivingTuesday is serendipitous. Even though I've previously written about the history of #GivingTuesday ("Giving Leads to Inspiration," *Teammate Tuesdays Volume II*, Chapter 31), I feel an obligation to highlight the occasion again since it involves several important good teammate qualities—kindness, generosity, and a willingness to sacrifice for the greater good.

#GivingTuesday aims to unite the world in doing good through giving. For some, the concept can seem overwhelming because they mistakenly interpret *giving* to equate to financial contributions—something they may not be able to give.

But #GivingTuesday isn't limited to making financial contributions. As it states on the organization's website, "Everyone has something to give and every act of generosity counts."

So what can *you* give? Can you give your time to someone who's overburdened? Can you give labor to someone who's incapable? Can you give companionship to someone who's lonely? Can you give a smile to someone who's sad? Giving any of those would be a *good teammate move* on your part.

I have a sign sitting on the bookshelf in my office that features one of my favorite quotes: "Your talent is God's gift to you. What you do with it is your gift back to God."

The quote is from Leo Buscaglia, and although there is no connection between Buscaglia and #GivingTuesday, his words capture the occasion's spirit.

Known by many as "Dr. Love" or "Dr. Hug," due to his propensity for embracing strangers, Buscaglia was a fascinating individual. His appearances on PBS in the 1980s were wildly popular and accounted for a considerable portion of public television's fundraising efforts.

Buscaglia dedicated his life to understanding what love is and how we can all embrace it. His interest in the topic evolved from the suicide of one of his favorite students while Buscaglia was a professor at the University of Southern California.

The tragedy moved Buscaglia to start teaching a non-credit class called "Love 1A" that focused on exploring the meaning of life and self-actualization. Hundreds of students sought enrollment in the unique class every semester, making it the university's most in-demand offering.

Buscaglia subsequently embarked on a successful speaking career and authored fourteen bestsellers. The aforementioned quote about talent comes from his fourth book, *Living, Loving & Learning*.

It's human nature to underestimate our talents, especially those that we don't necessarily think of as talents. Being able to run fast, jump high, or sing on key are readily acknowledged talents. But so should be the ability to patiently listen while the lonely ramble on about topics that are of little concern to us or the ability to recognize when the hurting need a comforting hug.

#GivingTuesday is growing to become as big a part of the peripheral holiday season as Black Friday and Cyber Monday. If we're lucky enough, the concept of giving selflessly of our talents to those in need will one day be ingrained in the fabric of our society.

As always…Good teammates care. Good teammates share. Good teammates listen. Go be a good teammate.

**Details about #GivingTuesday are from https://hq.givingtuesday.org/. Details about Leo Buscaglia are from a June 13, 1998* New York Times *article about his life (https://www.nytimes.com/1998/06/13/arts/leo-buscaglia-tv-advocate-of-love-s-power-dies-at-74.html).*

Good Instead of Great

DECEMBER 8

Sometimes I am asked why I use "good" teammate instead of "great" teammate. That's a *great* question.

The simple explanation has to do with the origins of my children's book, *Be a Good Teammate.* At the time of its writing, my oldest daughter had just started kindergarten and was learning to read using sight words.

If you're unfamiliar with the term, sight words, or Dolch words, are a collection of common words that children learn to recognize without sounding out the letters. My daughter's teacher had sent home a list of sight words they were learning in class and I tried to include words from that list in my book.

So, the simple answer is that "good" was on my daughter's sight word list and great wasn't.

I continue to use good, however, for more abstract reasons. As time passed, I realized that good provides a better representation of the type of individual to whom I am referring.

Great implies varying degrees of aptitude. In other words, how skilled are you? Comparatively, good is more binary. Good is on/off. Good is like being pregnant—either you are or you aren't. There is no sliding scale.

Either you consistently act in accordance with what is best for your team, or you don't. If you do, you meet the expectation and can be considered a good teammate. If you don't, you can't.

For some, that standard is hard to embrace. They don't want to think of themselves from a binary perspective. They prefer a sliding scale because they know they act in accordance with what is best for their team *occasionally*, *some of the time*, or *most of the time*. But not *all the time*.

Team members who fall into this category lean toward situational assessments. They tend to measure their actions based on how others behave, as opposed to holding themselves accountable to the standard.

Being a good teammate means you choose the option that is best for your team, regardless of personal preference, self-interests, inconvenience, or comfort zones. And you choose that option every time you have a choice.

Being a good teammate is a process. It's OK to be a work in progress as long as you continue to attempt to uphold the standard.

An ancillary benefit of using good instead of great is that, psychologically, people are more apt to try to pursue good. Right or wrong, the possibility of being great can seem too overwhelming. Good sounds much more attainable. Anybody can strive for good, which is fitting because anybody can be a good teammate.

As always...Good teammates care. Good teammates share. Good teammates listen. Go be a good teammate.

Making Others Whole

DECEMBER 15

The holiday season blesses us with several stories that embody the good teammate approach. Among my favorites is the story of the Christmas oranges. A few different variations of this story exist, but they all end the same way and contain the same heartwarming message.

Patricia Polacco's version, *An Orange for Frankie*, revolves around the Stowell family's holiday tradition of decorating their mantelpiece with evergreens and fresh oranges, which the children eat on Christmas Eve.

Even though Frankie, the youngest of the nine Stowell children, was told not to touch the oranges, he can't resist taking his down from the mantelpiece. When Frankie hears his mother entering the room, he hides his orange in his pocket to keep from getting in trouble.

But Frankie forgets about putting the orange in his pocket and loses it on the ride home from the Christmas pageant. Later that evening, while explaining to his mother why his orange is missing from the mantelpiece, Frankie confesses to giving his new sweater to a shirtless hobo earlier in the day.

Though disappointed with his losing the orange, Frankie's mother assures him that giving his sweater to someone in need was noble and in keeping with the true Christmas spirit.

Frankie accepts that he will not be able to participate in the family's tradition this year and heads downstairs. Upon his arrival, his siblings hand him an orange with a ribbon tied around it. Frankie quickly realizes the ribbon is holding together eight individual wedges and that each of his siblings' oranges is missing a wedge.

The story of the Christmas oranges contains a valuable "good teammate" reminder: You don't have to be whole to make someone else whole.

Sometimes people hesitate to give of themselves for fear of losing their worth. But giving a portion of yourself to someone in need does not diminish your worth; it magnifies your value.

To be a good teammate, you must be mindful of your actions and understand that actions that seem trivial to you may be monumental to someone else. Likewise, problems that seem monumental to you may be trivial to someone else.

Allowing yourself to be consumed with your life's problems can lead you to mistakenly thinking you're not able to make a difference in someone else's life. But that isn't necessarily the case.

Your life doesn't have to be perfect to help others. You don't need to have all your ducks in a row or your stars aligned to be a difference maker. Small sacrifices, kind gestures, and encouraging words are accessible to both the perfect and flawed.

The great miracle of service is that by helping others, you inescapably help yourself. Service, like the ribbon around the orange wedges in the story, binds team members to each other. When you have the potential to make a teammate whole again, act without hesitation.

As always…Good teammates care. Good teammates share. Good teammates listen. Go be a good teammate.

Ten Good Teammate Holiday Traditions

DECEMBER 22

As has become our Teammate Tuesday holiday tradition, no heavy reading this week. Instead, we kindly offer you a lighthearted, good-teammate-themed Christmas list.

Here are ten Christmas traditions with good teammate undertones:

1. **Giving gifts**
Generosity is a trademark of good teammates. They give fully and freely of themselves. And whenever there seems to be nothing left to give, they always manage to find a way to give a little more.

2. **Baking Cookies/Cookie Exchange**
Good teammates know the key to connecting with their fellow team members is getting into their hearts. As the saying goes, the way to the heart is through the stomach.

Baking and sharing cookies creates meaningful connections.

3. **Elf on a Shelf**
Elves are selfless servers. They epitomize what it means to be good teammates. The Elf on a Shelf experience sets everyone up for cherished memories.

4. **Christmas Caroling**
Blessed are those who can carry a tune. Talent is a gift to you, what you do with it is your gift to others. Using your talents to bring others happiness is crucial to being a good teammate.

5. **Salvation Army Bell Ringers**
Individuals who sacrifice their comfort for the benefit of others are good teammates. Having to endure holiday crowds and the repetitive sound of a ringing bell, while standing for hours at a time—often in the blistering winter cold—makes those manning the red Salvation Army kettles bona fide good teammates. (…and dropping donations in those red kettles is good teammate move!)

6. **White Elephant/Dirty Santa**
Whatever you call it, the game where participants take turns selecting and "stealing" impractical gifts delivers amusement. Good teammates are called to be good sports, and this game is an exercise in being a good sport and being happy for someone else's good fortune.

7. **Angel Trees**

Good teammates provide care to those who are unable to care for themselves. Sharing with the less fortunate, without the expectation of getting anything in return for your charity, is standard operating procedure for good teammates.

8. **Watching Christmas Movies**

Shared experiences bring teams closer together. Yucking it up over the brilliance of Clark Griswald's exterior illumination, Marv and Harry's follies, or Ralphie shooting his eye out is guaranteed to bond your team, as are any of the feel-good Hallmark movies.

9. **Sending Cards**

Social media may have diminished the prominence of this tradition but receiving cards in the mail is still fun. The joy they bring to others—especially those who are not on social media—far outweighs their inconvenience. Good teammates are willing to sacrifice their convenience for the benefit of others.

10. **Reading Stories**

Whether it's reading Dickens' *Christmas Carol* or *'Twas the Night Before Christmas,* gathering around the family patriarch or matriarch for a good Christmas story warms the soul and brings listeners closer together. By being good listeners, good teammates allow others to share.

From our team to yours, Merry Christmas! And, as always…Good teammates care. Good teammates share. Good teammates listen. Go be a good teammate.

The Year in Review

DECEMBER 30

We've been fortunate to build a loyal following on social media and have seen that following grow again this year. Our "teammates" enjoy the inspirational thoughts we post each day, and we enjoy sharing the message.

Many followers have found our daily posts to be an opportunity to refuel their good teammate tanks, rediscover purpose in their lives, and refocus their energies. If you know of someone who could benefit from a dose of the Good Teammate message, please encourage them to join the conversation and start following us on social media. They can connect with us on the following sites:

Facebook: *https://www.facebook.com/coachloya*
Twitter: *https://twitter.com/coachlanceloya*
Instagram: *https://www.instagram.com/lanceloya*
LinkedIn: *https://www.linkedin.com/in/coachloya*

In keeping with our annual *Teammate Tuesday* tradition, here are the posts from each of the past twelve months that received the most interactions, impressions, shares, likes, favorites, and retweets:

JANUARY

"Good teammates must be patient with everything except toxic behaviors from others. You must have an intolerance for toxic behaviors that disrupt your team's culture—and a willingness to confront those who do. #courage"

FEBRUARY

"Good teammates must have the ability to be happy for another teammate's success."

MARCH

"It doesn't take talent to be a good teammate, but being a good teammate is a talent."

APRIL

"Good teammates know that life is too important to be wasted on jealousy. Be happy for others' accomplishments."

MAY

"Good teammates do not require supervision. They can be trusted to exceed expectations because they are committed to their team's success."

JUNE

"Simple rule for team success: Good teammates find a way to make those around them better. WE>ME."

JULY

"Holding on to anger will hold you back. You can't be bitter and be a good teammate. Let it go!"

AUGUST

"Good teammates focus fully on whatever it is they are doing. Halfhearted-ness isn't in their character."

SEPTEMBER

"Good teammates go out of their way to not inconvenience others, yet they never mind being inconvenienced by something that will help their team be successful."

OCTOBER

"Take action! The needle is moved by your actions, not your thoughts."

NOVEMBER

"Want to make a difference on your team? Inspire others to believe in their significance."

DECEMBER

"Good teammates don't compete against each other. They compete for each other."

We hope you will continue to support our Good Teammate efforts, as we strive to reach a larger audience and inspire even more individuals to become better teammates. The world cannot have too many good teammates. Here's to a prosperous new year!

As always...Good teammates care. Good teammates share. Good teammates listen. Go be a good teammate.

A Messy Canvas

JANUARY 5

The beginning of a new year is often viewed as a prime opportunity to initiate change—a fresh start with a blank canvas. Got an undesirable habit? Make a resolution. Want to check something off your bucket list? Set a goal. Need direction in your life? Adopt a one-word theme.

Some people lack the courage to initiate change. Others simply put it off because they don't see themselves as being in a position to tackle the challenges of a new beginning. They think they have too much baggage, too many commitments, or too little time.

Their perceived lack of a blank canvas deters them from pursuing change. But that doesn't need to be the case.

Long before Bob Ross became a popular meme, he gained fame as the host of *The Joy of Painting*. Television audiences marveled at his talents. In less than thirty minutes, the iconic, afroed artist with the soothing voice could paint an entire landscape.

Interestingly, Bob Ross never started his projects with a blank canvas. He utilized a technique known as wet-on-wet painting in which layers of wet paint are applied to previously administered layers of wet paint.

In the opening of every episode, Bob Ross informed viewers that a "thin coat of liquid white" had already been applied to his canvas. What may have appeared to be a blank canvas was in actuality a wet, messy canvas.

Bob Ross blended the wet layer into his art. The messiness became part of the process. It gave his art depth and character.

You don't need a blank canvas to initiate change. Life is filled with inherent messiness. Your schedule isn't likely to ever be blank. You'll always have baggage and other commitments to contend with. Don't allow that premise to deter you from pursuing change. Find a way to blend the messiness of your life into the process.

Bob Ross had several popular sayings, including: "There's nothing in the world that breeds success like success." That quote applies to the ripple effect of change. One individual choosing to be a good teammate can change a team's entire culture.

Demonstrating the courage to initiate change in your life can trigger change in others. When you rid yourself of undesirable habits, accomplish goals, or embody your life's theme, you inspire those around you to do the same.

If you're still searching for a resolution/goal/theme for this year, consider making a commitment to be a better teammate. I promise, it will be a decision that you will never regret.

As always...Good teammates care. Good teammates share. Good teammates listen. Go be a good teammate.

Connected Mates

JANUARY 12

On January 15, 1892, *Triangle Magazine* published an article titled "A New Game." Written by a young physical education instructor from the Springfield School for Christian Workers (now Springfield College) named James Naismith, the article detailed the rules for a game the instructor had introduced to his students the previous month.

Sports enthusiasts will recognize the historical significance of this event as the first official publication of the original thirteen rules of basketball.

While there have been some alterations over the years, most of the game's original rules still apply. I've always been intrigued by Naismith referring to his new game as "basket ball" (two words) in the *Triangle Magazine* article and in his original handwritten notes.

At some point, the words basket and ball were connected to form the single moniker that we now use: basketball. Who made the decision to connect the words?

I have a similar curiosity about the word teammate. In both cases, the connecting of the words seems appropriate. The objective of the game is to connect the basket and the ball. The objective of those participating in the game is to connect themselves to their team—or at least it should be.

Good teammates buy in to their team's culture. They don't see their identity as being separate from their team's. They see the identities as being one and the same and relish the opportunity to integrate themselves into the team.

This is why good teammates don't have compliance issues. They adhere to team policies. They follow the proper procedures. They wear their uniforms the way they are supposed to be worn. Good teammates want to be connected to the team and are willing to sacrifice a portion of themselves for that happen.

The final pages of the *Triangle* issue containing Naismith's "Basket Ball" article include a variety of advertisements for nineteenth century goods and services—bicycle repair, camera shops, gymnasium equipment, etc. Nestled among those advertisements is a message thanking the magazine's subscribers.

The message reads as follows: "To those of you who have stood by us in our infancy and have aided us…we shall endeavor to give you the very best that can be procured." When you assess yourself as a teammate, do you feel that you *endeavor* to give your team the very best that you can procure? Good teammates do.

As always…Good teammates care. Good teammates share. Good teammates listen. Go be a good teammate.

A Little More Pixie Dust

JANUARY 19

This past weekend, I had the privilege of watching my daughters take the stage in *Peter Pan*. My oldest daughter was cast in the role of Peter Pan and my youngest played Tiger Lily. How well they and their castmates performed made my heart smile.

I anticipated leaving the theatre with an idea for a *Peter Pan*-inspired blog about some aspect of being a good teammate. Up until the play's closing moments, it didn't seem like that was going to happen.

Peter Pan is a fun story, but there simply aren't a lot of good teammates in it. The lost boys, the pirates, the natives, the Darlings, and Tinker Bell all tend to pursue self-serving agendas. They routinely choose "me over we" and give little thought to how their choices impact others.

I had all but abandoned the possibility of getting a blog topic from the show, until a slight miscue sparked an idea. In the play's final scene, Peter Pan returns to Wendy's window where he discovers Wendy to now be grown up, married, and with a child of her own. Peter convinces Wendy's daughter, Jane, to come with him to Neverland. The two of them are supposed to then "fly" out the window to end the play.

But something backstage caused the timing to be off with the crew operating the flying apparatus. Peter covered the delay by telling Jane, "Maybe you just need a little more pixie dust."

And with those words—*a little more pixie dust*—the inspiration I was looking for presented itself. In my book *The WE Gear*, I refer to good teammates as the magical ingredient in every successful team. Quite often, what makes good teammates magical is their ability to add *a little more pixie dust* to other team members.

They do this by being encouraging. Most people notice when a team member is struggling. Some rejoice in that misery. Others mind their own business and say nothing. Good teammates soothe the struggle by offering meaningful encouragement.

If their initial encouragement isn't enough, good teammates go back and offer a little more encouragement. It may not seem like a big deal, but to the downtrodden a good teammate's encouraging words can be the difference between flying and failing.

Frustration will ground a person's spirit and make that person want to quit. Phrases like *you can do it, don't give up*, and *I believe in you* are the equivalent of pixie dust because they have the same uplifting effect. They elevate others' confidence and encourage others to rise above the frustration.

Being a good teammate doesn't require any magical talents. All you need is faith, trust, and to share a little more pixie dust.

As always…Good teammates care. Good teammates share. Good teammates listen. Go be a good teammate.

Emancipate the Suck

JANUARY 26

Every subculture has a collection of epigrams—colorful, pithy expressions that are too informal to be considered jargon, yet too common to be labeled as slang. These colorful expressions offer outsiders a glimpse into the subculture.

For example, the sports world uses the expression "the ball never lies" to explain the divine overturning of a controversial call.

If the referee calls a foul, but the shooter misses the free throw...*Hey, the ball never lies.*

If the referee calls a penalty, but the kicker misses the field goal...*Hey, the ball never lies.*

The military has a name for their collection of epigrams: milspeak. One of my milspeak favorites is "Embrace the suck." Soldiers use the gruff expression when faced with tasks that are simultaneously unpleasant and unavoidably necessary.

Cleaning the latrine *sucks*. Training in the hot sun *sucks*. Doing a police call (milspeak for picking up trash around the barracks) *sucks*. Yet all those tasks are vital to military operations and must be done. The best way to proceed is to acknowledge them for what they are and then move forward.

Possessing the mental toughness to engage in unpleasant, yet unavoidably necessary tasks influences team success. Sometimes being a good teammate means *embracing the suck*. But not always.

The dictionary provides three meanings for the verb embrace:

- To hold (in one's arms)
- To accept or support
- To include or contain

Two of those meanings apply to good teammates; one does not.

Good teammates accept the unavoidable necessity of unpleasant tasks. They understand that tackling those tasks will not be enjoyable, but that the tasks must get done. Their understanding of the situation allows them to support whoever assigned them the task and keeps them from being resentful of the assignment.

Good teammates include the unpleasantness in their journey. They view unpleasant tasks as being part of the process, which they value because it offers them the gift of experience and perspective.

Good teammates, however, do not hold onto the unpleasantness. They recognize it, push through it, and then they let it go. They do not allow themselves to be consumed by the unpleasantness.

Alternatively stated, good teammates embrace the suck…and then they *emancipate the suck*. They free it from their minds. Unburdening themselves of the negativity keeps them from wasting their time complaining or being bitter.

What suck do you need to embrace to be a better teammate? What suck do you need to emancipate from your mind to keep from being bitter?

As always…Good teammates care. Good teammates share. Good teammates listen. Go be a good teammate.

Groundhog Dazed

FEBRUARY 2

Does any holiday possess a stranger premise than Groundhog Day? Celebrants gather in the cold, pre-dawn hours to watch a weather-prognosticating rodent be plucked from his burrow by a man wearing a tuxedo and top hat.

If the furry fellow, affectionately known as Punxsutawney Phil, sees his shadow, winter continues for six more weeks. If he doesn't, an early spring is expected.

I grew up near Punxsutawney, Pennsylvania and have experienced the hoopla at Gobbler's Knob firsthand. It's a fun, festive atmosphere, but it isn't quite the same as it's portrayed in the Bill Murray movie.

For starters, the event doesn't take place in "downtown" Punxsutawney. Gobbler's Knob is located in a clearing on top of a wooded hill, several miles away from the town. Spectators must either park in town and walk there or catch a ride on a shuttle bus. The gathering is more akin to Bonnaroo or Burning Man or even Woodstock than a quaint town festival.

Thanks to the movie, the expression "Groundhog Day" has taken on a life of its own. It's now commonly used to describe the feeling of living the same day over and over again. There's nothing new to report. Life is just wear, wash, rinse, and repeat.

Individuals on a team can experience a similar feeling when they become complacent in their roles. They get accustomed to doing the same routine until they're eventually overtaken by apathy. I like to refer to this situation as being *Groundhog Dazed.*

You punch in and punch out. You do your job, but little to nothing more. Whatever passion you may have once had to expand your role or increase your contribution to the team has faded. You've become content to be complacent.

Being Groundhog Dazed keeps you from being a good teammate. Your complacency prevents the team from achieving true synergy. Good teammates don't allow themselves to become stagnant. They continuously seek ways to do more and become more—for their team.

If you find yourself or someone on your team feeling Groundhog Dazed, here are three strategies to combat the situation:

1. **Mix up your routine.** Enter the building through a different door. Park in different spot. Eat something different for lunch. Eat lunch at a different time. Introducing small changes to your regular routine can produce new stimuli and get you out of your rut and back to finding your groove.

2. **Schedule stimulating tasks on your calendar the way you would appointments.** The tasks could be something you've been meaning to do like call an old friend or something that could expand your skill set like listen to a new podcast. People tend to check off what is written on their calendar and put off what isn't. Get yourself unstuck by taking advantage of your innate desire to check items off your to do list.

3. **Find an accountability partner.** We all need a teammate who is going to pull us out of our burrow and keep us from seeing our metaphorical shadow. They don't have to wear a top hat, but they do need to be top notch in terms of helping you liberate yourself from complacency. Find someone who will help you hold yourself accountable.

Groundhogs are true hibernators. From late fall to early spring, they curl up in their burrows while their heart rate and body temperature plunge. When they emerge from hibernation, they are ravenous.

When team members emerge from being Groundhog Dazed, they should be driven by a hunger to be a better teammate.

As always…Good teammates care. Good teammates share. Good teammates listen. Go be a good teammate.

Sweetheart Appreciation

FEBRUARY 9

A degree of mystery surrounds the origins of Valentine's Day. Historians can't agree on how or when the holiday began, or even who its namesake is.

Some believe the holiday was named after a martyred priest named Valentine, who in the third century defied a Roman decree outlawing marriage. Emperor Claudius II thought single men made better soldiers than married men with families, so he declared the sacrament of marriage illegal throughout the empire. When the Emperor discovered that Valentine had continued to conduct marriage ceremonies in secret, he had the priest beheaded.

Others believe Valentine was a wrongfully accused prisoner who fell in love with his jailor's daughter. Legend has it that the prisoner wrote the girl a final letter before he died that closed with the words "from your Valentine."

While we may never know the holiday's true origins, we do know that at some point Valentine's Day became *the* occasion to celebrate love—romantic or otherwise.

If you've got a teammate who you love being around or who loves being around the team, use Valentine's Day as occasion to convey your appreciation to that individual.

Buy them flowers, send them a card, or maybe gift them some candy. If you choose to go the candy route, consider Sweethearts—those tiny, chalky, heart-shaped, rock hard wafers. They aren't particularly tasty, but the messages stamped on them are endearing, if not comical.

Spangler Candy, Sweethearts' manufacturer, announced that this year they were adding twenty-one extra messages to the wafers. In addition to the usual BE MINE and HUG ME offerings, each box of sweethearts will include new messages inspired by popular love songs.

Since both Valentine's Day and being a good teammate are rooted in love, here's a lighthearted take on how the twenty-one song title messages Spangler chose (and a few of those songs' lyrics) apply to the art of being a good teammate:

IGOTU BABE (Sonny and Cher)
Good teammates got your back. When you're struggling, you can always depend on them. *When you're sad, they're a clown. And if you get scared, they're always around.*

SUGAR SUGAR (The Archies)
Being on a team with good teammates *makes your life oh*

so sweet! Doesn't take much to be left with *wanting more*—of their kindness, compassion, energy, etc.

CRAZY NLUV (Beyonce and Jay-Z)
How can you not be crazy in love with how good teammates make you feel? They empower you with confidence and make you feel safe to express yourself. *Yessir, they're cut from a different cloth.*

PER FECT (Ed Sheeran)
You'll see your future in their eyes. Good teammates are the *perfect* addition to any team, so perfect that you too are often left feeling like you *don't deserve* them.

SUMMR LOVIN (Grease Soundtrack)
Sometimes we don't realize how much we appreciate our good teammates until they're gone. Don't take their presence for granted, tell them how much you appreciate them before your relationship is *ripped at the seams.*

LOVE SHAK (The B-52's)
Love rules on teams with good teammates. When you love your team, you embrace your role. *Everybody's movin', everybody's groovin'* on teams that put WE ahead of me.

STILL THE 1 (Shania Twain)
Ain't nothin' better than beating the odds together. Good teammates are loyal. They will stick by your side through the best and worst of times. Good teammates make

people who say *I'll bet they'll never make it* eat their words.

ADORE YOU (Harry Styles)
Good teammates will *walk through fire for you.* They will go out of their way to help any team member in need. They refuse to allow inconvenience to determine the depth of their commitment.

LUVME TENDR (Elvis Presley)
Good teammates choose their words wisely. They have a gift for being *tender* when delivering bad news and tactful when confronting team problems. They *make your life complete.*

AT LAST (Etta James)
Anyone who's ever been on a team embroiled with selfishness knows how joyous it can be to at last join a team comprised of good teammates. The experience leaves you feeling like *your lonely days are over and your life is a song.*

1000 YEARS (Christina Perri)
Good teammates show you *how to be brave.* Their example gives you the confidence to love the journey without being *afraid to fall.* They make *all your doubts suddenly go away.*

ALLMY LIFE (K-Ci & JoJo)
You too will *praise the Lord above for sending* you a good teammate. They have the ability to fill the void in your life and become the reason you *turned your life around.*

MY GIRL (BOY) (The Temptations)
Good teammates make you feel like you've *got sunshine on a cloudy day*. Their positive attitudes influence your mood in a good way. They give you *so much honey* (praise, support, encouragement, etc.) that the bees *envy you.*

BABY LOVE (The Supremes)
Good teammates will never *treat you bad* or *leave you sad.* Their unwavering support and encouragement are like a *warm embrace*. They make you feel valued.

ONLY YOU (The Platters)
Good teammates make you feel special. They're attentive when you speak and genuinely happy for your success. They definitely make your *world seem right*, and *the darkness bright.*

HAPPY 2GTHR (The Turtles)
Good teammates think about their team *day and night.* Their undying loyalty fosters a culture of commitment and facilitates others' happiness. *You and them* are indeed *so happy together*.

I'LLBE THERE (The Jackson 5)

Just call their name and they'll be there. Good teammates will drop whatever they're doing to come to the aid of a fellow team member. They don't object to being inconvenienced for the good of the team.

I'M YOURS (Jason Mraz)

Good teammates humble themselves to serve the teams' needs. Their hearts and souls belong to their teams. *And if you look into their heart, and you'll find love, love, love, love.*

ALL OF ME (John Legend)

No need to question the depth of a good teammate's commitment. They are ALL IN and *will give their all to you.* They put every ounce of their blood, sweat, and tears into pursuing team success.

LEAN ON ME (Bill Withers)

When you're not strong or when you need a hand, you can always lean on good teammates. They will support you during your most challenging times and *help you carry on.*

10000 HOURS (Dan & Shay and Justin Bieber)

Good teammates are invested in their teams. They wouldn't hesitate *to spend ten thousand hours, and ten thousand more,* if that's what it takes to learn how to better serve the needs of their team.

If nothing else, the above list provides you with the makings of a good Valentine's Day playlist. From our team to yours, Happy Valentine's Day.

As always…Good teammates care. Good teammates share. Good teammates listen. Go be a good teammate.

**Details about the history of Valentine's Day and its patron saint are from https://www.history.com/topics/valentines-day/history-of-valentines-day-2*

***Details about the Sweetheart additions are from Spangler Candy's official website: https://www.spanglercandy.com/our-brands/sweethearts*

Measure Twice, Cut Once

FEBRUARY 16

Shop class used to be a staple in high school curriculums. Students learned how to use tools and build projects with their hands. For some, the class was an introduction to basic carpentry. For others, it was training for a future vocation.

The first day of every shop class in the world began with the same safety lecture: No horseplay, always wear safety goggles, make sure tools are unplugged before adjusting them, etc.

After students began to work on their projects, instructors would typically offer them an additional nugget of wisdom: *Measure twice, cut once.*

The fact that the wisdom was dispensed by an instructor who might be missing a finger or two didn't devalue its merit. *Measure twice, cut once* wasn't about safety; it was about certainty. Once a board was cut, there was no going back. If a mismeasurement caused a board to be cut shorter than it needed to be, that board could no longer be used. The student had to get another board, re-measure, and re-cut.

Mismeasurements were costly in terms of both time and money. Hence, it was better to be thorough and double-check measurements *before* cutting the board. The minor inconvenience of being thorough saved students and instructors a lot of aggravation.

Measure twice, cut once is the sort of transcending, sage advice that can also be applied to other aspects of life. The advice definitely applies to the art of being a good teammate. The words we use to communicate with the other members of our team matter. Choosing the right words can empower and inspire them. Choosing the wrong words can cut them as deep as any saw.

Far too many relationships have been unnecessarily damaged by words spoken in haste. Once words are spoken, they can't be taken back. Sure, you can apologize and try to subsequently explain what you meant to say, but that is the equivalent of having to get another board, re-measure, and re-cut.

The speaking in haste/apology cycle is an inefficient communication method. Before good teammates speak, they measure their words. They weigh them, vet them, and assess the extent of their potential impact. The minor inconvenience of being thorough saves them a lot of aggravation.

Measuring your words requires more than just thinking before you speak. You must rehearse before you speak—internally. Take a moment to say the sentence to yourself before saying it aloud.

How did hearing those words make you feel? How will they likely make the intended recipient feel? Will the words you used produce your desired outcome? Can better words be chosen?

Our fear of silence can cause us to be self-conscious about the length of the pauses in our communication. But others don't notice our pauses to be nearly as long as we assume they do. The speed of thought is always faster than we realize.

Don't allow a misperceived awkward pause to prevent you from rehearsing what you intend to say before you speak. The milliseconds you devote to measuring your words can keep you from *cutting* your teammates in an unintended way. Every good teammate knows that preserving a relationship is much easier than repairing one. Measure twice, cut once.

As always...Good teammates care. Good teammates share. Good teammates listen. Go be a good teammate.

Being an Agent of Change

FEBRUARY 23

This is my two hundredth blog entry. That I have written that many entries is almost unfathomable to me!!!

Four years ago, my friend Wendy suggested adding a blog to my website. She thought it would be a good way for me to add meaningful content to a site that was, at that the time, more barren that it should have been. I figured that I would write maybe five to ten entries and move on to something else. Obviously, things played out differently. And I am glad they did.

Sometimes readers will ask me which entry is my favorite, which is comparable to asking a parent to choose their favorite child. I am incapable of singling out one as my "favorite," so we polled our subscribers.

We compiled a list of our top blogs, based on website hits, clicks, comments, mentions, likes, shares, forwards, interactions, etc., and asked subscribers which blog they liked best. After tabulating several thousand votes, the list was narrowed down to three finalists. Here is a brief synopsis and the key takeaway for each of the three:

"Don't Feed the Gators."
(*Teammate Tuesday's Volume I*, Chapter 19)
A Florida sign about feeding alligators translates into advice for dealing with toxic teammates. When you do anything but disagree with a toxic teammate's malcontent, you are feeding their toxicity. Gators=haters, and good teammates don't feed the "gators."

"You Gotta Read the Book"
(*Teammate Tuesday's Volume II*, Chapter 32)
A high school football team uses Lance's children book to create a team-first culture and win a state championship. Any coach can coach strategy. Good coaches coach players. Great coaches make coaching players to be good teammates part of their strategy.

"The Pooh Bear Statue"
(*Teammate Tuesday's Volume I*, Chapter 52)
A child's thoughtful gesture reveals a good teammate insight. The essence of being a good teammate lies in the continued willingness to do kind, generous acts that may seem like nothing more than a small inconvenience to the doer, yet often mean the world to the recipient.

Watching my blog grow has been beyond enjoyable. Last month, I received an email from a reader who said that I make her "look forward to Tuesdays." My heart smiled. I appreciate hearing from readers, whether it's a story about how something I wrote had a positive impact on their team or just a simple message letting me know that an entry was a "good one."

Two-hundred blogs has allowed me to create a helpful database of sorts of good teammate topics. If your team is struggling with a particular teamwork problem, you can use the search bar on my website to discover archived blogs that are relevant to that problem. For instance, a quick search for "listening" brings up nine results, including *Ten Ways to Be a Better Listener.*

I try to write my blog with two objectives: To inspire people to be better teammates and to help people find ways to inspire those on their teams to be better teammates. Why? Because I believe the world needs more good teammates.

Nearly every affliction affecting our society (e.g., school bullying, the drug epidemic, broken families, political shenanigans, etc.) comes down to people not being good teammates. Several recent news headlines have reminded me of this fact.

Those same headlines have also reminded me of the significance of a quote attributed to Mahatma Gandhi: *Be the change you want to see in the world.*

I love that quote and it has been a driving force behind many of my life's decisions. But Gandhi never said those words. *Be the change you want to see in the world* is a condensed, bumper-sticker version of what he said. Gandhi's actual words are much deeper:

> *"We but mirror the world. All the tendencies present in the outer world are to be found in the world of our body. If we could change ourselves, the tendencies in the world would also change. As a man changes his own nature, so does the attitude of the world change towards him. This is the divine mystery supreme. A wonderful thing it is and the source of our happiness. We need not wait to see what others do."*
>
> – *Mahatma Gandhi*

To be a bona fide agent of change, you must look within yourself. You must ask yourself daily: Am I being a good teammate? Am I inspiring others to be good teammates? Affirmative answers to those questions are the key to discovering true happiness.

As always…Good teammates care. Good teammates share. Good teammates listen. Go be a good teammate.

**The above Mahatma Gandhi quote is from The Collected Works of Mahatma Gandhi, Volume XII, April 1913 to December 1914 (The Publications Division, Ministry of Information and Broadcasting, Government of India., 1964), 158.*

Your Emergency Is Our Emergency

MARCH 2

A red flag goes up whenever I walk into an office and see a sign hanging on the wall that reads: Your problem does not equate to my emergency. This sign makes me shake my head because it is a clear indication of a me-first/team-second culture.

I've seen several different variations of this sign—*Your poor planning is not my emergency*, *A lack of planning on your part does not constitute an emergency on mine*, and the overtly sarcastic *Let me drop everything and work on your problem.* None of these variations are particularly welcoming.

When I see this sign, I feel compelled to ask two questions, the first being: Why isn't their problem your emergency?

Good teammates are invested in their teams. They view their teammates' problems as their problems. An emergency is simply a problem wrapped in urgency. Hence, good teammates view their teammates' emergencies as their emergencies.

Being unwilling to equate a teammate's problem to your emergency violates the good teammate code of putting the team ahead of yourself. Nobody enjoys being inconvenienced. To have your work disrupted by others' problems, especially ones of their own making, is not pleasant. But enduring the inconvenience is necessary if helping them is what's best for your team.

The second question I feel compelled to ask is: What happened that necessitated the hanging of that sign?

It would be cavalier to not also consider the issue from the opposing perspective. Maybe the person who hung the sign is a selfish grouch whose attitude needs adjusted, or—more likely—they're someone whose past kindness was taken advantage of.

Being unwilling to equate a teammate's problem to your emergency may violate the good teammate code of putting the team ahead of yourself, but so does being inconsiderate of others. If your actions routinely inconvenience other team members, then you need to re-evaluate your methodology.

Does a variation of one of the aforementioned signs hang in your office? Consider taking it down and adopting instead the mindset of an emergency room physician.

Every patient who comes to the emergency room has a problem. The emergency room physician's job is to help them with those problems. The physician doesn't resent the patients for having problems, object to being inconvenienced, or get annoyed by how many patients come into the emergency room with problems.

Sometimes the physician must weigh the urgency of the patients' problems. Gunshot wounds and heart attacks are more pressing than sprained ankles. But the physician is receptive to helping with every problem and helping every patient.

Emergencies are rare occurrences. Fifty individuals may come into the emergency room with the same problem on the same day. But if the same individual comes in with the same problem for fifty days, then it is no longer a matter of urgency. It's a matter of competency.

To provide the same type of care to that patient wouldn't be helping them; it would be enabling them. Good teammates don't enable bad behaviors. They confront them. In this case, the best way to help the patient would be to bring the issue to the attention of someone who has the authority to put an end to their behaviors.

If you have teammates on your team who see your emergencies as their emergencies, make sure you reciprocate their kindness. Make sure you also recognize and reward it. And most importantly, make sure you don't take advantage of it.

As always...Good teammates care. Good teammates share. Good teammates listen. Go be a good teammate.

How to Handle Being Betrayed by a Teammate

MARCH 9

"Beware of the Ides of March." The soothsayer offers this warning to Julius Caesar in Shakespeare's play of the same name. Caesar fails to heed the warning and is later assassinated on the Roman Senate floor. Before dying, Caesar utters the equally memorable, "Et tu Brute?" (You too, Brutus?)

That Caesar spoke those exact words is doubtful. "Et tu Brute" is forged from Shakespeare's creative genius. While historians suspect Caesar's dying words were something along those lines, no one is really certain. What we can be certain of, though, is that Caesar was surprised by Brutus' betrayal.

Brutus was Caesar's trusted friend and protégé. Caesar had done much for Brutus, which made his betrayal especially hurtful. For that matter, Caesar had done much for many of the other conspirators who participated in the assassination. He had granted several of them clemency for crimes against the empire only weeks before they (quite literally) stabbed him in the back.

Being betrayed by someone is a hard to accept—especially when that someone is a trusted teammate. How do you handle a teammate who betrays you?

In an ideal setting, the best option may be to simply move on and distance yourself from that teammate. But that option isn't always available. Sometimes you have no choice except to keep working alongside the teammate who betrayed you. What do you do when this is the situation?

- **Influence the Perception**

  You probably won't be able to force a retraction or get the offending party to admit fault. Even if you could, whatever was said or done has already happened and is beyond your control. The proverbial horse is already out of the stable.

  Focus your energy instead on conducting yourself in such a way that nobody would believe whatever falsity was said about you and everybody will believe that you were wronged. Allow your example to outshine the darkness that was thrust upon you.

- **Forgive**

  In my book *The WE Gear*, I describe good teammates as individuals who shift their attention from *me* to *we* when they come to clutch moments in their lives. They choose what's best for the team over what's best for them individually. Forgiving the person who harmed you may be what's best for your team—even if that person doesn't offer an apology or feel sorry.

Abuse counselors remind patients that forgiveness is about the offended, not the offender. As an old adage advises: Holding on to anger is like grasping a hot coal with the intent of throwing it at someone else; you are the one who gets burned. Holding onto anger can cause you to become bitter and distracted. Both of those behaviors lead to a toxicity and are never what's best for you or your team.

- **Don't Feed the Gators**

This comes from a Florida sign about alligators. Treat haters (those who criticize, betray, and are otherwise negative towards you) the same way the sign directs people to treat gators. Haters hunger for negativity, so don't feed them any.

Spreading retaliatory gossip about them, treating them rudely, giving them the silent treatment, or engaging in any other pettiness intended to avenge your betrayal feeds their negativity. Take control of the situation by choosing to be above the pettiness.

If you've been betrayed by a teammate, be cognizant of the possibility that they believed they were acting in the best interests of the team. Before condemning their actions, consider that what you perceived as betrayal could be a misunderstanding between differing perspectives.

Also, understand that those willing to stab others in the back to get ahead have "broken transmissions." They are too self-centered to be able to shift from the me gear to the we gear. You don't have to be sympathetic to their brokenness or take it personally. But being empathetic to their condition can reduce the sting of their betrayal.

As always...Good teammates care. Good teammates share. Good teammates listen. Go be a good teammate.

You Have One Job

MARCH 16

The "you had one job" memes never disappoint. They provide some of the best laughs because they are absurd—yet laced with truth. The expression is the perfect response to seeing such blunders as handrails installed in the wrong direction of a stairwell, mislabeled produce, or misspelled key words on a sign.

One of my personal "you had one job" favorites comes from Hong Kong airline Cathay Pacific. When their newly painted 777 emerged from the hangar, the letter "F" was conspicuously missing from the plane's paint scheme.

While I suspect Cathay Pacific's leadership wasn't laughing at the costs required to fix the blunder, the airline's social media account at least had some fun with it, tweeting that the plane will be "going back to the shop."

As far as blunders go, misspelling the company's name on a jumbo jet is a pretty big blunder. It is precisely the sort of mistake that makes us pause and wonder: *You had one job, how did you manage to fail so badly?*

"You had one job" memes are the result of someone's carelessness. What was asked of them wasn't especially difficult. The blunder simply evolved from them not giving their job its due diligence.

They either didn't pay attention to what they were doing or didn't care enough about the task to be thorough in assessing its quality. The optimum word being *care.*

When you're part of a team, you have a responsibility to care. And when you're part of a team, you have one job: Be a good teammate. How often team members fail at that job is equally laughable.

Team members pursue self-interests ahead of team interests, prioritize individual agendas over team goals, and routinely engage in behaviors like gossip that are detrimental to their teams' wellbeing. Each of those transgressions equate to good teammate failure.

We don't give those responsible for the failures in the "you had one job" memes a pass, nor should we give team members who fail at their sole responsibility a pass. Being a good teammate isn't as complicated as some try to make it out to be. All that's essentially required is a commitment to be the best versions of yourself—*for your team.*

This commitment manifests in how you think, speak, and act. When you convey respect for your team's culture, you're doing your job. When you show loyalty to your team's leadership, you're doing your job. When you sacrifice individual wants for team needs, you're doing your job. But when you act selfishly, you're failing at your job.

The next time you see the word Batman printed on a Superman backpack or a mug handle attached to the inside of the mug, before you laugh at someone's failure to do their "one" job, think about the sort of teammate you've been. Have you been living up to the expectations of your "one" job?

As always…Good teammates care. Good teammates share. Good teammates listen. Go be a good teammate.

Countering Donor Fatigue

MARCH 23

Anyone who works in fundraising is familiar with the concept of donor fatigue—a situation that develops when donors stop giving to a cause they previously supported. Donor fatigue can cripple an organization whose operations depend upon benefactor generosity.

What causes donors to stop giving? Did they lose interest in the cause? Are they being inundated with requests? Do they no longer have funds available to donate?

All those reasons are viable possibilities. Part of working in fundraising is figuring out the reason for donors disengaging and then developing a plan to counter that disengagement. This approach requires fundraisers to become *invested in their investors.*

Fundraisers must consider what they did, or perhaps failed to do, that facilitated their donor's disengagement. Did they take their donor's generosity for granted? Did they fail to recognize their donor's generosity? Did they allow their donor's emotional connection to the cause to go stale?

People are generally the most committed to causes where they have an emotional connection. Someone who lost a loved one to cancer is more likely to donate to a cause related to cancer. The parent of a diabetic child is more likely to donate to a cause related to diabetes research. Alums who had memorable experiences are more likely to donate to their alma mater. Emotional connection compels investment.

Good teammates will sometimes encounter their own version of donor fatigue. Only the issue isn't from the fundraiser's perspective; it's from the donor's perspective.

Having your kindness unrequited, your sacrifices unappreciated, or your loyalty unrewarded can wear you down and leave you feeling fatigued. You wonder if trying to be a good teammate is worth the hassle. Your efforts start to seem pointless and you begin to feel the urge to disengage.

If you find yourself in this position, the solution is to revisit your *why*. Ask yourself: "Why am I conveying kindness, making sacrifices, and showing loyalty?"

Something compelled your initial commitment. Whatever did so is your *why*—and just like the charity's donors, you probably have an emotional connection to your *why*.

Donors, whether they be donors of financial support or donors of kindness, sacrifice, or loyalty, experience fatigue when they forget the reason behind their contribution: their belief in the cause. They need to periodically remind themselves why they believe in their team's mission.

Good teammates don't allow themselves to be discouraged by instances of unrequited kindness, unappreciated sacrifices, or unrewarded loyalty because they are invested in their team's mission. Good teammates are driven to be kind, make sacrifices, and be loyal because they believe those are the right choices to make.

If you're making the right choices, don't allow yourself to become fatigued. Revisit your *why* and keep fighting the good fight. Be aware, though, that not everyone on your team has the same level of insight as you and/or may not be as driven as you. Ward off those team members' potential for experiencing donor fatigue by openly recognizing their kindness, sacrifices, and loyalty.

Doing so will be a revitalizing good teammate move on your part.

As always...Good teammates care. Good teammates share. Good teammates listen. Go be a good teammate.

Don't Be Afraid to Care

MARCH 30

Pink Floyd released its iconic album, The Dark Side of the Moon, forty-eight years ago this month. Considered by many to be one of the greatest concept albums of all time, it still holds the world record for the most weeks charted on the Billboard Top 200.

The Dark Side of the Moon examines the themes of conflict, greed, and time in relationship to mental health. It focuses on what Pink Floyd front man Roger Walters describes in a documentary about the making of the album as elements that "make people mad (crazy)" and the "importance of empathy."

The album's title alludes to the once common belief that lunacy—insanity—is connected to the moon's lunar cycles, with the "dark side" being the most volatile.

While progressive music was the source of The Dark Side of the Moon's success, at least a portion of the album's initial popularity stemmed from its unique cover art. Designed by

Hipgnosis associate George Hardie, the album cover shows a prism refracting a light beam.

Good teammates are a lot like prisms. When light enters a prism, it is transformed into a more pleasing array of beautiful colors. Metaphorically, the same happens to toxicity when it enters a good teammate.

Toxic entities like greed, jealously, and resentment lead most people to complain, criticize, and shift blame—responses that amplify problems and cripple team morale.

Good teammates transform problems into opportunities to grow. Instead of complaining, criticizing, or wasting precious time attempting to shift blame, good teammates concentrate on finding solutions. They turn toxicity into felicity—the state of being happy.

The opening verse of the second track on The Dark Side of the Moon, a song called "Breathe," contains a line that is pertinent to the art of being a good teammate: Don't be afraid to care.

The fear of rejection, of being hurt, of being embarrassed, of appearing vulnerable, or of not having actions reciprocated can keep team members from investing in team problems. Good teammates aren't deterred by these fears because their decisions aren't governed by fear; they're guided by love.

When confronted with a problem that threatens their teams' culture, good teammates become invested in the problem and commit to seeing it resolved. How do they do this? By having the courage to care. They take on problems that discourage others, out of love for their team.

Different colors of light travel at different speeds. Red light travels faster than violet. Orange travels faster than blue. As white light (the presence of all colors) travels through the medium of a prism, the colors are bent at different speeds and a rainbow of colors emerges on the other side. This process is known as the "index of refraction" and is why prisms work.

Just as different colors travel at different speeds so do the solutions to different problems. Some problems take longer to remedy than others. But when placed in the hearts of good teammates, every problem, including those that take the longest to remedy, eventually emerge as something more pleasing.

As always...Good teammates care. Good teammates share. Good teammates listen. Go be a good teammate.

Seven Things Good Teammates Do That Go Unnoticed...But Shouldn't

APRIL 6

Retired educators tend to remember the students who caused them problems yet forget the ones who did not. Why educators remember difficult students is understandable. Those students gave them more stress and usually occupied more of their time.

But for the students who didn't cause any problems to be overlooked is unfortunate. The "good" students followed directions, adhered to rules, and conformed to expectations. They made their instructors' jobs easier by doing things that are appreciated, but often unnoticed.

Good teammates are similar in that they too engage in beneficial behaviors that go unnoticed. Here are seven things good teammates do that go unnoticed—but shouldn't. (And by *shouldn't*, I don't mean that good teammates shouldn't engage in these behaviors; I mean their behaviors shouldn't go unnoticed. These behaviors are all deserving of recognition.)

1. **They listen to others' problems.** Pent up frustrations lead to busted pipes. Good teammates lend a receptive ear to those who need to vent. They curb their teammates' emotional outbursts by allowing themselves to be sounding boards.

2. **They remember important details.** Good teammates remember birthdates, anniversaries, and other special milestones. They also remember details about their teammates' problems. If the information is important to their teammates, it is important to them.

3. **They make connections.** Good teammates are connectors. They are intentional about connecting their acquaintances with each other for their acquaintances' benefit. Their motivation to make these connections comes from their desire to help others.

4. **They acknowledge good deeds and good work.** Good teammates don't take either of those entities for granted. When another team member engages in praise-worthy actions, good teammates acknowledge their actions with open praise and appreciation.

5. **They provide levity.** Good teammates lighten the mood of stressful environments through laughter and, occasionally, self-deprecating humor. Their humility

permits them to laugh at themselves and not be offended by others laughing at their follies.

6. **They elevate others' self-esteem.** Good teammates are gifted at making the person with whom they are speaking feel special. They endear others by empowering them with confidence. Rare is the occasion when you leave a conversation with a good teammate and not feel better about yourself.

7. **They discipline themselves.** Good teammates espouse the John Wooden mantra of disciplining yourself, so others won't have to. Having to deal with wayward team members diverts the team leaders' time and keeps them from focusing on more impactful endeavors.

If you've got someone on your team who engages in any of the above behaviors, don't allow them to go unnoticed. Express your appreciation and do your best to facilitate their continuance.

As always...Good teammates care. Good teammates share. Good teammates listen. Go be a good teammate.

Carlos the Car Care Specialist

APRIL 13

My work with corporate teams often centers on improving customer service. Business leaders want their employees to work together and for there to be harmony in their workplace, but they *need* their employees to be teammates—*good* teammates—to their customers to maximize profits.

When employees view customers as their teammates rather than necessary burdens, they convey higher levels of loyalty, empathy, commitment, and appreciation. They become invested in their customers' problems and are far more likely to go out of their way to help resolve those problems.

I try to share examples of superior customer service anytime I encounter an employee who espouses good teammates standards. I experienced one of these encounters last week while having my wife's car serviced at a local dealership. The employee's name was Carlos and his title was "car care specialist."

The days of people taking their car to a garage and interacting with a mechanic in greasy overhauls are going by the wayside. Today, taking your car to be serviced is more like a trip to the doctor's office. You schedule an appointment, you wait in a cushy lounge with televisions and refreshments, and you rarely speak to the actual mechanic. You deal instead with an intermediary known as a car care specialist.

Car care specialists are liaisons between the mechanic and the customer, and the best have superior bedside manner. Like great doctors, they are skilled at delivering bad news.

I brought my wife's car to the garage to have a routine oil change and tire rotation. She wasn't having any problems with her car, so I didn't expect to need any other work done. Carlos approached me in the waiting room and said, "I can tell you've been taking good care of your car. We got the oil changed and tires rotated, but I think you also need an alignment.

"Your tires are wearing kind of funny. If we do an alignment, you'll probably be able to get another thirty to forty thousand miles out of them. But if we don't, I suspect you'll be back in here in a couple of months needing new tires and experiencing some bigger problems."

Nobody wants to receive bad news, especially when they're not expecting it. Effectively communicating negative information and getting a positive reaction requires skill.

Carlos confronted me the way good teammates confront problems with other team members. He approached me and gave me the "sweet" (*I can tell you've been taking good care of your car*). Then he gave me the "sour" (*I think you also need an alignment*).

He followed that up by presenting the benefits of what would happen if I acted upon his recommendations (*you'll be able to get another thirty to forty thousand miles out of your tires*) and the consequences of not acting upon them (*you'll be back here in a few months needing new tires*).

Had Carlos summoned me to him and informed me that I needed more work done, I would have been skeptical of his motives and questioned the necessity of that work. By approaching me, tactfully presenting the problem, potential benefits, and consequences, he created an atmosphere of trust and improved the likelihood of me accepting what he had to say.

Despite receiving *unexpected* news that required *unexpected* repairs and *unexpected* expenses, I drove away from the dealership in a good mood. Carlos' pleasant disposition and effective communication were a big reason for this. Carlos isn't known as a "car care specialist" because of his intimate knowledge of cars; he's known by that title because of his ability to make the cars' owners feel special.

Sometimes team members fall out of alignment. They lose focus, act counter to the team's culture, and need their attitudes adjusted. When this happens, good teammates must step into the role of "team care specialist" and help misaligned team members get re-aligned.

As always...Good teammates care. Good teammates share. Good teammates listen. Go be a good teammate.

Regret-Free Endings

APRIL 22

No one has a more insightful perspective on life than those nearing its end. Experiencing the final sands trickle from life's hourglass permits the dying a unique position of reflection.

For the past thirteen years, Tenzin Kiyosaki has served as an interfaith hospice chaplain at Torrance Memorial Medical Center in Los Angeles, California. She wrote a book about her experiences counseling hospice patients who have less than six months to live titled *The Three Regrets.*

In the book, Kiyosaki outlines the three most common regrets she hears hospice patients express at the end of their lives:

1. I did not live my life dreams.
2. I did not share my love.
3. I did not forgive.

When I read Kiyosaki's list, an immediate thought came to me: *Good teammates don't have those regrets.*

Good teammates experience challenges, failure, and heartbreak the same as everyone else, yet when their hourglasses run out of sand, they are at peace with themselves. They aren't haunted by regrets, unresolved issues, or bitterness because their lives have been guided by a simple formula: *Service leads to purpose. Purpose leads to happiness. Happiness leads to wholeness.*

Serving the needs of their team allowed them to live a purpose-driven life, filled with happiness. When dreams are stripped of materialism and boiled down to their most basic premise, dreams are about achieving happiness. Biochemically, the human body does not differentiate between the happiness that comes from marrying the person of your dreams, landing the job of your dreams, owning the house of your dreams, or traveling to the destinations of your dreams.

In other words, living a happy life equates to living your life dreams.

Sharing is a basic tenet of being a good teammate. Good teammates share every element of their existence: possessions, time, knowledge, and—of course—love. They never withhold their love nor pass on opportunities to convey it. Hence, they have no regrets about sharing their love.

The same is true of forgiveness. A conscious commitment to being empathetic lets good teammates forgive. They don't hold grudges nor hold onto anger. They forgive transgressions (including their own) and move on without regret.

The metaphor of sands running out of an hourglass isn't exclusive to the end of life. That metaphor can apply to the end of a game, the end of a season, the end of a career, the end of a relationship, etc. For good teammates, every one of those situations ends with a feeling of inner peace—because they know they did their best *for their teams.*

Tenzin Kiyosaki has seen the difference between individuals who approach the end with agitation compared to those who approach the end with peace of mind. Her motivation for writing her book and sharing her discoveries is to help people become more aware of the inevitable arrival of "the end" and to encourage people to live a life free of the three most common regrets.

My motivation for sharing this chapter is to help you realize that being a good teammate is how you steer clear of those regrets. Life's hourglass cannot be turned over and started again. But you can change the quality of sands that flow through your hourglass at any point by choosing to enjoy the journey and doing your best to be a good teammate for however long the journey may last.

As always…Good teammates care. Good teammates share. Good teammates listen. Go be a good teammate.

Bring the Good Teammate Message to Your Team

Are you interested in bringing the "Good Teammate" message to your event or implementing strategies to improve the quality of the teammates you have on your team? If so, contact Lance Loya at:

Phone: (814) 659-9605

E-mail: info@coachloya.com

Website: www.coachloya.com

Twitter: @coachlanceloya

Facebook: facebook.com/coachloya

Instagram: @coachlanceloya

LinkedIn: linkedin.com/in/coachloya

Join the movement and sign up for Lance Loya's weekly *Teammate Tuesday* blog at *www.coachloya.com/blog.*

*If you have enjoyed this book or it has inspired you in some way, we would love to hear from you! Be a good teammate and share your photos and stories with us through email or social media. We want to hear from you!

About the Author

Lance Loya is the founder and CEO of The Good Teammate Factory. As a leading authority on team dynamics, he specializes in getting individuals to shift their focus from *me* to *we*. Other experts concentrate on improving teamwork, but Lance concentrates on improving the teammate. Lance's method works!

Lance has authored eight books on the subject of being a good teammate, including *The WE Gear*, which made *Forbes'* list of "20 Books to Make You a Better Coach or Mentor."

A college basketball coach turned author, blogger, podcaster, and professional speaker, he is known for his enthusiastic personality and his passion for turning *teambusters* into good teammates. Lance has inspired readers and audiences around the globe through his books, keynotes, and seminars.

When not speaking or writing, he is a loyal husband to his high school sweetheart and a doting father to his two daughters—who, incidentally, were the impetus behind his heartwarming children's book.

Also by Lance Loya

Be a Good Teammate

An illustrated children's book teaches the importance of teamwork and how to be a good teammate. Good teammates care, share, and listen. You don't have to play sports to be on a team. This book encourages kindness and counters bullying.

Building Good Teammates

The story of Lance Loya's discovery of an alternative approach to coaching players to be good teammates explores how his personal Mount Rushmore—the four men who had the biggest impact on his life—and a quirky nun influenced his coaching methodology.

Teammate Tuesdays

In this compilation of the entire first year of Lance Loya's popular weekly blog of the same name, each chapter examines a different aspect of being a good teammate. Gain insight and encouragement through a variety of "good teammate" observations.

Teammate Tuesdays Vol. II

Go deeper into the world of good teammates in this compilation of another entire year of Lance Loya's popular weekly blog of the same name. Includes *musings* ranging from touching stories to creative ideas for inspiring team members to become better teammates.

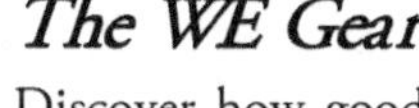

The WE Gear

Discover how good teammates shift from *me* to *WE*. Everybody wants teamwork on their team, but teamwork does not happen without good teammates—individuals whose unique way of thinking propels their team to success no matter what team they are on.

Teammate Tuesdays Vol. III

In this third installment of the *Teammate Tuesdays* series, Lance Loya once again chronicles a year of his journey exploring what it means to be a good teammate. Fifty-two weeks of observations unfold through fifty-two short, easily digestible chapters.

Outside the Box, Within the Cube

Be inspired by this collection of 1,001 quotes about the art of being a good teammate. Quotes motivate us to become better versions of ourselves. They lift us up when we feel down, guide us when we feel lost, and empower us when we feel constrained.

The Good Teammate Podcast

Listen to Lance Loya explore the art of being a good teammate in audio selections from his *Teammate Tuesday* blog. You can also download past episodes and subscribe on Apple Podcasts, Spotify, or Google Podcasts.

www.coachloya.com/podcast

Learn from a Course

The Good Teammate Factory offers online video courses to help teams gain greater insight in the art of being a good teammate. Courses are available for both sports and corporate teams and are an ideal way to improve teamwork, reduce selfishness, and draw teams closer together.

Teams engage in the course content and activities together in a group setting such as a meeting room or classroom. The courses are flexible in that they can be completed in a single sitting or divided up and stretched out over a series of meetings.

If you want to improve teamwork, send your team to The Good Teammate Factory!

WWW.GOODTEAMMATEFACTORY.COM

Take the Quiz

Are *you* a good teammate? Your team's potential for achieving success is ultimately dependent upon your answer to this question. Everybody wants teamwork on their team, but teamwork doesn't happen without good teammates—individuals who prioritize team objectives over personal agendas.

Gaining insight into the kind of a teammate you are increases your awareness for how your actions impact the other members of your team. It also increases the likelihood of your team working together to achieve genuine synergy.

Take the good teammate quiz today to assess your aptitude for practicing good teammate behaviors! To learn more about the quiz, visit:

www.coachloya.com/quiz/

www.ingramcontent.com/pod-product-compliance
Lightning Source LLC
LaVergne TN
LVHW050640100826
845148LV00011B/1922

9781737088905